THE MIRACLE TABLE

REDISCOVERING THE POWER OF COMMUNION

BY ANDREW MURRAY

The Miracle Table

Copyright 2018 Andrew Murray

No part of this book may be used or reproduced in any matter without the written permission of the author. This book may not be reprinted without permission from the author.

All Scripture quotations unless otherwise indicated are taken from the Holy Bible, New International Version® Anglicized, NIV® Copyright © 1979, 1984, 2011 by Biblica, Inc.®
Used by permission. All rights reserved worldwide

Scripture taken from the New King James Version®. Copyright © 1982 by Thomas Nelson. Used by permission. All rights reserved.

The Passion Translation®. Copyright © 2017 by Passion & Fire Ministries, Inc.
Used by permission. All rights reserved. thePassionTranslation.com

Scripture taken from The Message. Copyright © 1993, 1994, 1995, 1996, 2000, 2001, 2002. Used by permission of NavPress Publishing Group.

Holy Bible, New Living Translation, copyright © 1996, 2004, 2015 by Tyndale House Foundation. Used by permission of Tyndale House Publishers, Inc., Carol Stream, Illinois 60188. All rights reserved.

Common English Bible, Copyright 2010 Common English Bible Committee

Scripture quotations marked NJB are from the New Jerusalem Bible, Darton, Longman and Todd and Les Editions du Cerf, Copyright 1985

Scripture quotations taken from the Amplified® Bible (AMP),
Copyright © 2015 by The Lockman Foundation
Used by permission. www.Lockman.org

Published by Generation Builders

Book designed and formatted by Laura Murray at Peanut Designs www.pnutd.co.uk

CONTENTS

Pre-face		10
Introduction		15
1.	The Great Longing of God	21
2.	Welcomed, Accepted and Changed	33
3.	Remembrance – The Invitation Into Encounter	47
4.	Remember – The Covenant	63
5.	The Communion Encounter (Part One)	79
6.	The Communion Encounter (Part Two)	93
7.	The Table – The Place of Transportation	109
8.	The Table – A Place of Transformation	125
9.	The Table – Where I Fight My Battles	141
10.	A New Order	161
11.	Shadows of the Christ	175
12.	Koinonia	197
13.	The Table – The Place of Ecstatic Joy	211
14.	The Table – A Place of Extravagant Worship	223
15.	Hungry and Thirsty For Jesus	233
Conclusion: The Miracle Table		239
Afterword: Seeing Jesus		

Acknowledgements

My beautiful wife Laura

Judah and Asher – my boys

The rest of the Murray family – mum and dad, Matthew, Becky and Josiah

Jarrod and Vicky Cooper – our incredible senior leaders. We love and honour you

Our Revive Church family. What a community to be part of!

Our wonderful friends – Lucy (from Hull!), Steve and Ané, Jonathan and Lamia.

Dave and Carolyn, Cleddie and Gaynell

All our friends and supporters from around the world

The Generation Builders trustees – Kevin and Janet, Nigel and Angie, Steven and Sharon, Peter and Anna

Samuel Dent for proof reading and correcting

I am grateful for J. Todd Billings for his book "Remembrance, Communion and Hope: Rediscovering the Gospel at the Lord's Table" for some great historical background on the history of the Breaking of Bread.

Dedication

To Judah, my firstborn. My great prayer for you is that God would give you a hunger for Jesus and a thirst for His presence. May you always know what it is to feast from the Master's Table.

"I was poor in the midst of riches, and ready to perish with hunger near a table plentifully spread and a continual feast. Oh, beauty, ancient and new! Why have I known thee so late"

- Madam Guyon

Preface

Why write a book about Communion? I suppose it is out of frustration. As I read the Scriptures, firstly I find the importance that Jesus and the early church placed upon the Communion meal. Secondly, I find the great power and blessing that is available for God's people as they gather around the Lord's Table. In addition to the Scriptures, as I read into church history I find incredible encounters people had during the Breaking of Bread. For hundreds of years, the place of Communion has been a special place of divine encounter, and divine exchange.

What frustrates me is that I seldom see this power and these encounters taking place in our modern day Communion services.

I have been brought up in Church my whole life, and always attended churches where Communion was taken, if not weekly, then at least every month. I have been in hundreds of Communion services. In recent years as I have travelled as an evangelist I have attended churches all over the world that have taken Communion in a variety of different ways.

Very rarely I have been in a Communion service where I have seen the true power and glory of God manifest as we have broken bread. Sadly I have often found that the time around the Lord's Table has become repetitive, boring, and devoid of any real supernatural power. This should not be the case. As I study the Bible and Church history, I am convinced that there is an untapped well of power and life contained within the Breaking of Bread.

On occasions when I have taught on Communion, and some of the principles found in this book, I have seen believers have their eyes opened and approach the Table with a freshly discovered sense of awe and expectancy. This has resulted in powerful times around the Lord's Table, often with healings and miracles breaking out. It is my prayer that this becomes the norm in all our Communion services.

I am often asked questions like, "How often should a local church break bread?" and "What should we do on a practical level to make our times of Communion more powerful?"

I must admit I don't have those answers. This is not a practical book, it is a revelatory book. It is down to each individual church to allow the Holy Spirit to show them how often they should take Communion and what they should do around the Lord's Table.

But the "when" and "how" are secondary questions. The most important question is "why." The question this book attempts to answer is the "why." Why should we come around the Lord's Table? I believe that as we discover the "why" all the practical details will figure themselves out.

Why do we come around the Lord's Table? To remember? Yes, but more than that. There is a communion within the Communion. And that is what this book is about. In some ways, the act of coming around the Lord's Table whether that be once a day, once a week, once a month, or even once a year is not important. It is about a lifestyle of truly communing with God, and fellowshipping with the Holy Spirit - this is what the Table speaks to us about. That is the heart behind this book - that we would draw close to God, and truly discover what it means to know Him.

You will notice that throughout this book I have included quotes from several of what we would call the 'early church fathers,' and 'Christian mystics.' I make no apologies for this. These men and women had a depth in their revelation of the Lord's Table that very few have today. I do not agree with everything they wrote or all of their theological positions, but I want to learn from men and women like this, and discover the revelation of fellowshipping with God at the Table that they had.

One thing that will become apparent to those reading this book is my use of 'prophetic types' that I believe are found in the Bible. This way of interpreting the Scriptures was used by Jesus and by Paul. I believe that one of the reasons we struggle to put fresh language around the Communion experience is that we limit the texts we draw from to the account of the Last Supper and Paul's teaching in 1 Corinthians. However, when we begin to read the Bible prophetically we see that the language of Communion - bread and wine, the cup, the table, the feast, and eating and drinking - this is all the way through Scripture, and opens up our understanding with a new depth and insight.

My prayer for all that would read this book is that you would see Jesus, and that you would be drawn into a place of deep communion and fellowship with the lover of our souls.

"The Eucharist is the consummation of the whole spiritual life."

- St. Thomas Aquinas

Introduction

"You prepare a table before me in the presence of my enemies." Psalm 23:5

In Matthew's account of the Last Supper he records that as Jesus broke the bread He "blessed it." (Matthew 26:26 - KJV) It is significant that when Jesus instituted the Communion meal He did so with a blessing. Later, when Paul is describing the drinking of wine at the Lord's Table, he describes the cup as "the cup of blessing." (1 Corinthians 10:16 - KJV)

I believe that contained within the act of Communion is the very blessing of God; and the blessing that was spoken by Jesus over the bread and wine still rings out two thousand years later. When we eat the bread and we drink the cup, we are eating and drinking over that which Christ Himself has blessed. We are doing something that has been blessed by Him and in doing so we are receiving the blessing of God.

"Take, eat; this is My body which is given for you." (Matthew 26:26 – KJV) He gives and we take. He blesses and we receive. He has done it all, He has spoken the blessing, He has given His life. Now our response is in faith to eat and drink, and in doing so to receive His blessing and to appropriate it as ours.

In Genesis 27, Jacob, dressed as his brother Esau approaches his elderly father Isaac with the purpose of receiving his blessing. The blessing that Isaac gave his son is significant for us as we re-discover the power that there is in Communion:

> *'May God give you of heaven's dew and of earth's richness - an abundance of grain and new wine.' (Genesis 27:28)*

The blessing that the father speaks over his son is that he would receive an abundance of grain (bread) and wine. Later when Jacob's deception is revealed, Esau comes to Isaac and begs for a second blessing. Note Isaac's response:

> *'I have sustained him (Jacob) with grain and new wine. So what can I possibly do for you, my son?' (Genesis 27:37)*

Jacob and Esau both recognised the necessity of having their father's blessing. They knew that it was the greatest thing that they could possess. In turn Isaac recognised that the greatest blessing that he could give his son was an abundance of bread and wine. When Jacob was blessed with these things, Isaac knew that there was nothing greater that he could give to Esau. The greatest, most powerful blessing was contained within the bread and wine.

The greatest thing that any of us can possess is the blessing of our Heavenly Father. To have His blessing on our lives, our finances, our marriages, our children, and our ministries, is the greatest thing that we can possess.
God's greatest blessing is found at the Communion Table within the Bread and Wine. The Communion Table is God's greatest gift to His people because that is where His blessing is found. The ultimate blessing is found in the Bread and Wine because the Bread and Wine speak of Jesus - His Body and His Blood - and in Him is every spiritual blessing. (Ephesians 1:3) There can be no greater blessing than to dine with Him, and to dine of Him.

> *'You prepare a table before me.' (Psalm 23:5)*

> *'Go and make preparations for us to eat the Passover.' (Luke 22:8)*

Jesus lovingly and tenderly prepares this feast for us. Nothing is left to chance – all that we desire, long for, and need has been prepared for us. There is truly an abundance of bread and an abundance of wine which speak of the abundance of His blessings that have been laid out for all of us to receive.

'Martha was distracted by all the preparations that had to be made.' (Luke 10:40)

Martha's error was thinking that it was her job to make the preparations. Mary understood that the Master has already made the preparations - our job is simply to sit at His feet and commune with Him, trusting that He has already finished the work. I cannot add to what He has already done. My job is just to believe it and receive it.

God's blessing of grain (bread) and wine is something that is repeated throughout the Old Testament. Only with a New Covenant understanding can we see that this blessing is found in Christ, in His Body and Blood.

Joel 2 is another example of this blessing that God speaks over His people:

'I am sending you grain, new wine and oil, enough to satisfy you fully.' (Joel 2:19)

It is important to note that along with the grain and the wine, a third element is introduced - the oil. Several times in the Bible, the oil is mentioned alongside the grain and wine. Another example is Jeremiah 31:12:

'They will come and shout for joy on the heights of Zion; they will rejoice in the bounty of the Lord - the grain, the new wine and the olive oil, the young of the flocks and herds. They will be like a well-watered garden, and they will sorrow no more.'

The oil speaks of the precious anointing of the Holy Spirit.

Not only is there a blessing contained within the Bread and Wine but there is also an anointing available there too.

> *'You prepare a table before me in the presence of my enemies.*
> *You anoint my head with oil; my cup overflows.' (Psalm 23:5)*

The anointing of the Holy Spirit is there in the Communion meal. The anointing is found at the Lord's Table. It is the anointing of God that breaks the yoke of the enemy. (Isaiah 10:27) It is the anointing of God that brings freedom, healing, and restoration. (Luke 4:18) It is the anointing of God that empowers us for service. (Acts 10:38) It is the anointing of God that releases true joy. (Hebrews 1:9) It is the anointing of God that leads us into knowledge of the truth. (1 John 2:20) It is the anointing of God that enables our lives to overflow with the goodness and mercy of God. (Psalm 23:6)

This anointing is found right here at the Table of the Lord.

The anointing of the Holy Spirit is wherever Jesus is, and Jesus is always at the Table. He is the Master of the Banquet, and He is the Banquet. He is the One who offers the bread and wine, and He Himself is the bread and wine.

In Genesis 18, Abraham and Sarah invite three men into their home. They break bread and dine together. In the following chapter Abraham's nephew Lot encounters two of these men and he invites them into his home where he also breaks bread with them. Neither Abraham nor Lot realise that they are dining with angels. They are unaware that they are breaking bread with creatures from another world. In Abraham's case, one of the men that he was breaking bread with was Christ Himself.

Do we as the Church realise that as we break bread we do so in the very presence of God? Christ Himself is with us at this Table. For Abraham as he broke bread, God's prophetic purposes for his family were revealed and accelerated. For Lot, as he broke bread with angels, divine protection was released over his family.

Could it be that there is still an anointing and blessing that God wants to release over our homes and families as we rediscover the power of the Lord's Table? Could there be anything greater than to break bread in the presence of the Lord with our spouses and children? Could this release a new dynamic of the blessing and anointing of God over our families?

God never intended for the pulpit or the platform to be at the centre of His Church. For Him, it always was and always will be the Table. Human history began with a man and a woman enjoying communion with God in a Garden. Eternity will begin with the Perfect Man, Jesus, sat at a Table enjoying communion with His Bride. And right in the centre is this God Man, the One with nail scarred hands, sitting at His Table, and inviting us to commune with Him.

> *'I am the bread of life. He who comes to me will never go hungry and he who believes in me will never go thirsty.' (John 6:35)*

> *'Come, all you who are thirsty, come to the waters; and you who have no money, come, buy and eat! Come, buy wine and milk without money and without cost.'*
> *(Isaiah 55:1)*

"I am quite sure that if we could but once approach the most Holy Sacrament with great faith and love, it would suffice to make us rich. How much more if we approach it often!"

- St Teresa of Avila

1
THE GREAT LONGING OF GOD

"I have eagerly desired to eat this Passover with you before I suffer."

(Luke 22:15)

Imagine for a moment that you woke up one morning and you knew that you were about to die. Imagine that you woke up knowing that within hours you would be betrayed by one of your closest friends and abandoned by everyone else who claimed to love you. Imagine that you knew that you were about to suffer horrific torture and die the most agonising of deaths.

Faced with that scenario, I imagine we would face the day with distress, fear, and hurt at the forefront of our emotions.

I find it amazing then that when Jesus woke up that day, there was something that He was looking forward to! Jesus, knowing that He was about to go to the cross and suffer physical, emotional, and spiritual torment like no one else in history had ever faced, said that there was something on his "to do" list that day that He was longing to do. That was to have a meal with His disciples.

The Breaking of Bread, Communion, the Eucharist, the Lord's Table – this sacrament that came out of the Jewish Passover meal, was instituted by Jesus that day, and it reveals like nothing else the great longing and desire of God seen throughout the Bible – to have intimate fellowship with His friends.

The Great Desire

"I have eagerly desired" – feel the heart of Jesus as you read these words, He eagerly desired to have communion with His disciples. The Greek Word used here is epithumia, and it means 'to long for,' 'to lust after,' 'the setting of one's affections toward,' and 'setting the heart towards.'

This is the passion that Jesus had, and still has, to have communion with His disciples. Although faced with the prospect of an agonising death just a few hours later, in that moment all He longed for was to eat and drink with His followers.

Other translations of this verse help to show us the intense longing and passion in the heart of Jesus for communion. The New Jerusalem Bible says that He 'ardently longed for,' the Amplified says He 'earnestly wanted to eat this Passover,' the New Living Translation says He was 'very eager,' whilst The Passion Translation says 'He longed with passion and desire.'

The truth is that none of our translations can adequately describe the deep longing that Jesus has to have fellowship with His followers. Out of all the translations I still don't think that you can better how the King James put it, "He said unto them, "With desire I have desired to eat this Passover with you."'

"With desire, I have desired." This is the passion of the Christ. It began not at the cross, but at a table.

Last words, last actions, last moments – they are significant. They can become even more significant if you know in advance that they are going to be your last. Surely in that moment you would carefully plan exactly what you would do and say, wanting every second to be precious, and nothing be done without meaning. It says a lot of the priorities of Jesus that in His last hours He wanted to spend it eating and drinking at a table with those that He loved.

It is significant that the thing that Jesus instituted as His final act before the cross was not a church growth strategy, or a worship service outline - but a meal. Nothing speaks more of closeness, friendship, and companionship than people having a meal together.

The longing of God has not changed – it has always been for fellowship. When Mankind was created it was with the purpose to walk and talk with God in the Garden. Adam enjoyed a close, intimate relationship with His Creator, because it was why he was created. The story of the Bible is how Adam lost that communion with God, and how God did everything He possibly could to restore it.

The Book of Revelation describes the Second Coming of Jesus, declaring, "Blessed are those who are invited to the Wedding Supper of the Lamb," (Revelation 19:9). History ends with another table, another meal, another feast. When God restores everything and time is no more, He celebrates again with a communion meal – this time between a Bride and a Groom. It has always been and always will be about communion, relationship, and intimacy.

The Great Invitation

Jesus came not to institute a new religion but to usher in a new Kingdom – God's Kingdom, or the Kingdom of Heaven. He came declaring that the Kingdom of God was near, and that when we are born again we are born into that Kingdom. In Matthew 22, Jesus tells us what that Kingdom is like:

'The Kingdom of Heaven is like a king who prepared a wedding banquet for his son. He sent his servants to those who had been invited to the banquet to tell them to come.' (Matthew 22:2)

Once again, Jesus uses the analogy of a meal, a feast, a banquet to describe His Kingdom. The table is at the heart of His Kingdom and the focus of His invitation. He doesn't invite us to attend a stuffy religious service - He invites us to a meal table, a place of sweet intimacy and friendship.

Take note of the longing of the King for dining companions: Go to the street corners and invite to the banquet anyone you find. (Matthew 22:9)

There is still an invitation that goes out today; who will respond to the call of the King, who will come to His table?

'You didn't choose me, but I've chosen and commissioned you to go into the world to bear fruit. And your fruit will last, because whatever you ask of My Father, for my sake, He will give it to you!' (John 15:16 – TPT)

A straightforward reading of this Bible verse implies that Jesus primarily calls us to go and bear fruit as we advance His Kingdom. However in the Aramaic (the common language of Jesus' day) another meaning is revealed. Literally, 'I have invited you as my dinner guests and commissioned you to go into the world to bear fruit.' Jesus is calling us to a dinner table! This translation of this well-known scripture brings with it stunning implications for how we view Christianity. We now see that before we "go and bear fruit," we are first called to "come and dine." The going, and the fruit bearing is the overflow of our coming and dining, and fellowshipping with Him. The priority of our Christianity is not our service or ministry life but our table life. Only in first coming to the table and dining with Him are we able to be fruitful.

Our Response

In Matthew 22, those who were originally invited to the wedding banquet refused to come. They are not unique in their refusal to come and dine with the King. Even from the beginning, we find Adam and Eve hiding from God, running from the very thing that they were created for – communion. However, throughout the Bible there have been those who responded to the King's invitation to come and dine with Him.

70 Elders

Exodus 24 contains one of the most stunning encounters with God in the Old Testament. The context is that God enters into covenant with the nation of Israel. The covenant is then ratified through the shedding of the blood of sacrificed animals. Moses sprinkled the blood and declared "this is the blood of the covenant that the Lord has made with you" (Exodus 24:8)

What followed then is an invitation for four key leaders and the 70 elders of the nation to ascend into the very presence of God Himself. I wonder what they were expecting to find as they were beckoned to 'Come up to the Lord,' (v1). My guess is that they didn't expect to find a picnic! But that's exactly what they found, as 'they ate and drank' with God!

God celebrated the making of covenant not with a boring, dull, religious ceremony, but with a meal, with food and fellowship.

The Bible describes how in the context of this covenant meal they 'Saw the God of Israel,' (v9). The Hebrew word used here is ra'ah, meaning that they 'discovered' and 'experienced' God as they ate with Him. The New Jerusalem Bible states that they 'actually gazed upon God.'

This is the stunning grace of God, and the beauty of His invitation.
'Under His feet was something like a pavement made of sapphire, clear as the sky itself,' (v10) – the writer is painting a picture of a Majestic, Mighty King, and yet in His presence, there was no wrath or judgement. He 'did not raise His hand against these leaders' – but He invited them to sit at this table and eat and drink with Him as they enjoyed sweet fellowship together.

The phrase that they 'saw God' is used twice in these verses – verse 9 and also verse 11. Interestingly two different Hebrew words for 'saw' are used. Verse 9 is the word ra'ah which we have already looked at, but in verse 11 the Hebrew word hazah is used. This word means to see as in terms of a revelation or vision, but it is also used elsewhere in the context of prophecy.

As these leaders ate and drank with God, little did they realise that they were prophesying of another day when God would sit down and eat with man.
Once again it would be at the making of another covenant, but this time it would be One greater than Moses who would declare "this is My blood of the covenant, which is poured out for many." (Matthew 26:28) It is a better covenant, an eternal covenant, sealed not with the blood of animals, but with the precious blood of Jesus Himself.

But once again at the heart of the sealing of the covenant – an invitation to a meal, to communion with God.

<u>John the Beloved</u>

Another person who truly took hold of the invitation to have communion with Jesus was John, one of the twelve disciples. Famously at the Last Supper, John would lean back against Jesus as he reclined next to Him at the table.

In our modern understanding when we think of Jesus and His disciples eating the Last Supper, we often picture them sat in chairs and seated around a table. This is after all the image that Leonardo Da Vinci portrayed in his famous painting. However, the Bible is very clear that when Jesus and His disciples were at the table they were reclining. This was common practise in that culture – they would lie down reclining on a low couch. This would mean that the meal itself was incredibly relaxed and informal.

Now contrast this with our modern day Communion service! Communion is one of the most ritualistic, formulaic parts of our worship service. Even in more contemporary churches, or Spirit-led churches, they still have a pattern of how they take Communion. It leaves us with something repetitive, and dare I say, boring!

This is the total opposite as to what Jesus had in mind. For Him Communion was the most relaxed, informal, 'chilled out' time that He could spend with His disciples. It was less about being seated formally in rows, and more a group of friends, lying down, passing each food and drink, laughing, relaxing and enjoying each other's company. This is what Jesus intended all along.

If we are doing communion "right" then it should be the most relaxed, informal and spontaneous part of our worship service!

It is in this atmosphere that John 'the disciple that Jesus dearly loved…was leaning his head on Jesus.' (John 13:23 – TPT)

How close does Jesus allow us to get? As close as we want! John drew so close that He could feel the breath of Jesus on his neck, smell His fragrance and hear His very heart beat. This is the invitation we all have at the Lord's Table. We must understand that we also are the dearly loved of Jesus. He loves us with an unconditional, passionate, intense love, and He longs to have communion with us. With desire He desires for us to get so close that we feel His breath, smell His fragrance, and hear His heartbeat. He longs for us to get so close that we can gaze into His eyes and hear His very whisper.

Communion is an invitation to lean into Jesus. This immediately reminds me of three Bible verses:

> 'Israel worshiped as he leaned on his staff.' (Genesis 47:31)

Communion is an invitation to worship passionately as we lean on Him as our support, our faithful Father and friend.

> 'Trust in the Lord with all your heart and lean not on your own understanding.'
> (Proverbs 3:5)

Communion is an invitation to move away from our own understanding and our need to grasp everything that is happening, and like a child, just lean into His wisdom, trusting that He is in control and have an unwavering trust in His ways and goodness.

> 'Who is this coming up from the wilderness leaning on her beloved?'
> (Song of Songs 8:5)

Communion is an invitation into understanding that even in the wilderness of this world we are still His beloved and we can still lean into Him as our support. It is as we draw close to Him in communion that He gradually brings us up out of our wilderness and once again into a place of fruitfulness.

Sometimes in communion all that you can do is just lean in, throwing yourself upon Him. There is nothing that Jesus loves more than this. It is not very refined, not very cultured, not very respectful – but that was never what you were invited to, anyway! You were invited to take off your shoes and lie down. It's time for friendship.

The First Church

The early Church understood the desire of Jesus for communion and eagerly responded to His invitation.

Acts 2 describes the culture of the early church:

'They devoted themselves to the apostles teaching and to the fellowship, to the breaking of bread and to prayer.' (Acts 2:42)

It is amazing that in the 21st Century our churches can be filled with a hundred different activities. They aren't necessarily wrong activities, but in the early beginnings of the Church, they had just four major priorities: teaching, fellowship, prayer, and the breaking of bread. For the purpose of this book, we are of course focusing on the last one. The breaking of bread was a vital priority for the early church. It was something they 'devoted themselves' to and were steadfastly faithful in doing.

Now it is not for me to say how often a church should break bread. Some do it every service and it can be incredibly dead and dry, some can do it once a year and it can be the most powerful moment on their calendar. How often we do it and where we do it (in homes or larger gatherings) is surely an individual matter for each local church to be led by the Holy Spirit. But one thing is for certain, as the Church, the Breaking of Bread must be an absolute priority. It was for the first Church. They had responded to the invitation to dine at the King's table and recognised the great longing that God has always had for communion with His people.

It is a challenge to ask ourselves, if we were to list our top four priorities as local churches, would the breaking of bread make it? How about top ten?

What Went Wrong?

Just a few decades after we read about the first church in Jerusalem making Communion a passionate priority we read about another church: the church in Laodicea. In Revelation 3, Jesus writes to this church that is outwardly prosperous and successful; but this church that is so rich and comfortable has become lukewarm and complacent.

Staggeringly Jesus is not even in this church anymore, but is standing outside wanting to get back in! What is He wanting? – 'if anyone hears My voice and opens the door, I will come in and eat with him, and he with Me.' (Revelation 3:20)

He is wanting what He has always wanted – communion.

Amazingly, this rich and prosperous church had stopped having communion with Jesus! And they didn't think that it was that important!

Jesus uses very harsh words of rebuke towards this church, calling them "wretched, pitiful, poor, blind and naked," saying He wants to spit them out of His mouth and urges them to repent before He comes to remove their lampstand from its place.

This church is a sober warning for the modern day Church. Particularly in the West, we are so prosperous and comfortable. In our comfort have we also forgotten the vital importance God places on us coming and having communion with Him? Are we busy getting on with all our programmes and endeavours, not hearing the voice of the One knocking at the door, who desperately wants us just to recline at the table and eat and drink with Him?

Our priorities have changed, but Jesus' have not. He still longs and desires more than anything else to have communion with His Church. He still invites us to a table. He still knocks patiently at the door, gently reminding us of His promise, 'If you hear my voice and open the door, I will come in, and we will share a meal together as friends.' (Revelation 3:20 - NLT)

Prayer of Response

"Father, thank you for the incredible privilege that it is to come and eat and drink with You. I am humbled that the Creator of the heavens and the earth would invite me to dine with Him. I recognise that Your desire is for me, that you long to have fellowship and relationship with me. Father, I respond to your invitation. I come to Your Table and I lean into You. I worship You, I trust You, I acknowledge You. Father, in the midst of the busyness of life and in the midst of all the outward trappings of this world, let me never move from this place of sweet communion with You. Father, this is Your desire, let it be my desire also. I want to know You, to hear Your voice, to feel Your heartbeat. Draw me close to You. In the Name of Jesus. Thank you Father. Amen."

"Without shame and without doubt, eat the flesh and drink the blood if you are desirous of true life."

- *St. Gregory of Nazianzus*

2

WELCOMED, ACCEPTED, AND CHANGED

"While Jesus was having dinner at Matthew's house, many tax collectors and sinners came and ate with Him and His disciples."

(Matthew 9:10)

One of the most scandalous things about the life of Jesus was that He wasn't fussy about who His dining companions were!

For the orthodox Jew, who you ate a meal with was very important. Sitting down and eating food with someone was a sign of kinship, of friendship, and of goodwill. Eating with someone was a sign that you accepted them, and that if there were any issues between you, the meal was a token of peace.

Because of that, Jews were very careful who they ate with. Even today, we wouldn't just sit down and eat a meal with a stranger. The very act of sitting at a table with someone signifies some level of friendship and closeness. The Jews of Jesus' day felt even stronger about this. They certainly would never eat with Gentiles or people who were known to be breakers of the law.

If you were a religious leader like Jesus then you had to be especially careful who you ate with. You had to appear beyond reproach and a Rabbi or religious teacher would never risk the scandal of sitting down to eat with people who were known as immoral or "sinners".

But not Jesus! Not only did Jesus seemingly not care about who He ate with, but it seems that He specifically went out of His way to eat with those who society deemed the lowest of the low.

These were the law breakers, the immoral, the unclean, the liars, the cheats, the prostitutes – and they were all welcome at Jesus' table!

This was scandalous stuff, 'When the Pharisees saw this, they asked his disciples, "Why does your teacher eat with such scum?"' (Matthew 9:11 – NLT)

Thank God that Jesus still eats with those considered scum! Thank God that He still eats with sinners. Thank God that the dirty, the immoral, the law breakers are still accepted at His table. Thank God that He is still the friend of sinners.

We have a King who searches the streets and alleys looking for 'the poor, the crippled, the blind and the lame,' (Luke 14:21) and then gives them a seat of honour at His banqueting table. This is the very heart of the gospel!

That is where He found most of us, in darkness, in the broken places of this world. We were not angels when He found us, but we were sick and broken by our sin, bankrupt of any redeeming qualities. But still He found us, still He invited us, still He brought us to His table.

The scandalous love of Jesus! There is a place for anyone at His table!

One of the great lies regarding the Communion Table is that you cannot come and partake if you have sin in your life. I remember as a child in church, observing the grown-ups during the Breaking of Bread. On occasion I would notice that people would gesture that they didn't want to take Communion that week. On the way home I would quiz my parents who would say something like "they must have sinned this week!"

So my understanding was that if you had lived a holy life that week then you could take Communion, but that if you had sin in your life, you must not take it under any circumstances. After all, the Bible teaches that we are to examine ourselves before we take Communion and that anyone who eats and drinks in an unworthy manner risks the judgement of God!

But eating and drinking in an unworthy manner is not quite the same as an unworthy person eating and drinking. After all, who is worthy? Who is good enough? But that is the point. A God who says sinners cannot eat at His Table, is not the God revealed by Jesus Christ who specifically went out of His way to eat with sinners!

It is true that you are to examine yourself before you come to the Table. Chances are that you won't like what you see, but don't let that stop you eating and drinking. To do so is a denial of the gospel and the person of Jesus. No, come, your forgiveness is found at the Table! If your examine yourself and find sin, it doesn't mean your invitation is no longer valid. No, your sin is the very reason why you need to come to His Table in the first place!

This is the scandalous invitation of Jesus: Come liars and come cheats. Come adulterers. Come those battling lust. Come criminals. Come drunks. Come addicts. Come thieves. Come haters. Come liars. Come gossips. Come one and all. You are all welcome to eat and drink with Me at My Table.

For so many communion is a time of self-examination that leads to shame and guilt – I am not good enough to come to this Table. But whilst there is a call to repentance, it is not a call to "make ourselves ready" or "make ourselves worthy". Rather, it is acknowledging that I am a sinner that cannot change myself or make myself worthy, so I respond to the invitation of grace that allows me to dine with deity just as I am.

The greatest sinners during Communion are those who feel that their own righteousness has earned them a seat at the Table. The greatest grace is found for the ones who know that they are not worthy and yet respond to the invitation anyway, humbled and staggered that there is a place for sinners like them.

Perhaps no story better illustrates the acceptance that Jesus offers to all at His Table then the story found in Luke 7 of the woman who anointed Jesus.

A Sinful Woman

The Bible describes this woman as a 'sinful woman' who had lived a 'sinful life' and was known by all as a 'sinner.'

The implication is that this woman had lived a very immoral, sexually promiscuous life. She was probably a prostitute.

Can you imagine the guilt, shame, and feelings of unworthiness that this woman felt on a daily basis? Each day and night, as men touched her and did even worse things to her, imagine how dirty, and how unclean she felt.

And yet this woman did something that didn't make any sense unless she knew the reputation of Jesus. She came to His banqueting table.

'When one of the Pharisees invited Jesus to have dinner with him, He went to the Pharisee's house and reclined at the table. A woman in that town who lived a sinful life learned that Jesus was eating at the Pharisee's house, so she came there with an alabaster jar of perfume. As she stood behind Him at His feet weeping, she began to wet His feet with her tears. Then she wiped them with her hair, kissed them and poured perfume on them.' (Luke 7:36-38)

Can you imagine the boldness that it took to walk through that room, with every eye fixed on you? Some looking lustfully, some in judgement and scorn, others with hatred for what she represented. And she made straight to the Masters table.

At the dining table of Jesus, she wept, she showed her vulnerability, and she worshipped (in her own way), showing such love and tenderness. At the table she poured out all that she had.

The staggering confidence this woman had in coming to the table. Not confidence in her own righteousness, but confidence in His mercy. She trusted that His love and grace was so big that He wouldn't turn her away. She trusted that there would be a place for her at the table. She trusted that there wouldn't be judgement or condemnation but forgiveness and salvation.

This is the faith that saved her (Luke 7:50) – her faith in knowing that no matter who she was and what she had done, there was a place for her at the table.

"Your faith has saved you." Here Jesus uses the word sozo. Meaning, your faith in coming to the table has not only give you eternal security but it has made you whole, complete, with deliverance and healing. The same promise is for all who come to the Table, no matter who they are or what they have done. The word sozo can also mean "safety." For her and for us, the Table is a safe place. Not a table of judgement but a table of acceptance, forgiveness and restoration.

> *'When the Pharisee who had invited Him saw this, he said to himself, "If this man were a prophet, he would know what kind of woman is touching him. She's a sinner!"' (Luke 7:39)*

Of course, Jesus knew what kind of woman she was! He knew every man she had slept with, He knew every immoral act. He knew every thought, every secret, every shameful thing. He knew it all. He knew sins that they didn't even know about! Yet she had come to the table! And He never turns anyone away who comes to the Table!

The Pharisee's were up in arms! They just didn't get it! Religion never does. Even years later, the great church leader, Peter was afraid to eat with Gentiles because of what the religious would think, (Galatians 2:12). But Jesus would eat with anyone that was hungry.

If Jesus wouldn't disqualify you, how dare you disqualify yourself! Do you trust Him enough to come to the Table just as you are, believing that there is a place for you?

This woman's lips had kissed many men. But now they were kissing Deity, becoming intimate with holiness. And yet it didn't bother Him at all. Oh the mercy that there is at the Table!

At the table her "great debt" would be cancelled (v43) and she would hear these words "Your sins are forgiven." (v48)

Can you imagine the joy that flooded her soul at the sound of those words! Every sinful deed was now washed away in a wave of mercy. At that moment all guilt was lifted, all shame was wiped away. At that moment she was clean, she was righteous, and she was worthy. In that moment, she became the second most righteous person in the whole room!

Yet these are the same words that come to us from the lips of Jesus whenever we come to the Table. "No matter who you are, no matter what you are, and no matter where you have been or what you have done – you are forgiven!" It's all found at the Table!

On one occasion Jesus got a telling off from the religious leaders because His disciples didn't wash their hands properly before they ate at His table. It seems you can even come to His table with dirty hands and He doesn't care! It doesn't matter how you come, it matters how you leave.

How did this woman leave? 'Go in peace,' (v50). When did this woman last know peace? Had she ever known peace? When did she last lay her head on the pillow, knowing that she had peace with God? You can be certain that she did that night! She had been to the table of the Prince of Peace, and now perfect peace filled her heart, mind and soul. Oh that we would all find the peace with God that is found at the Table.

"Go…" she came to the table a sinner, but left having found a Saviour. There is something about the Lord's Table that has a transforming effect on our lives. Another wonderful example of this is found in the story of Zacchaeus.

A Sinful Man

Luke 19 tells us a few things about Zacchaeus that give us clue's as to what his life must have been like.

Firstly, he lived in a place called Jericho. If you read your Bible, you will read that Jericho was a city that had been cursed by God. God had cursed whoever rebuilt Jericho, and Ahab did just that, and it cost him the life of his first born son. So Zacchaeus lived every day in a cursed place, a daily reminder of God's judgement on the disobedient.

Secondly, we read that Zacchaeus was a tax collector, in fact he was the chief tax collector. This had made him very wealthy. And yet it had also made him deeply unpopular. As a servant of the Roman Empire, Zacchaeus was hated and despised. He was the kind of person, children would shout rude things at in the street, and to whom adults would cross over to the other side of the road as he walked by.

Can you imagine the loneliness Zacchaeus felt? The pain? The hurt? The rejection? The fear? The self-loathing?

Thirdly, we know that Zacchaeus was a sinner. Not in the general "we are all sinners" that we can quote theologically, but this guy really was a sinner! Everyone knew it! He was a liar, a cheat, a thief! Imagine the guilt and shame he felt. Imagine not being able to enjoy any of his wealth, knowing deep down that it had come from exploiting people.

Like Zacchaeus, we all live in the midst of a world cursed by sin, and the terrible effects of that sin affect us all daily. Like Zacchaeus we can all experience feelings like pain, hurt, loneliness, fear, and self-loathing. Like Zacchaeus we have all sinned and know the guilt and shame that are the consequences of our own selfish choices.

Yet like Zacchaeus, we have a choice today – we too can run to a tree! For Zacchaeus it was a Sycamore tree that he ran to and climbed. For us, it is the tree that Jesus was crucified on. It is at the tree where Our Saviour shed His blood that we find an invitation so humbling, so undeserved, so shocking – an invitation to dinner!

> *'When Jesus got to that place, He looked up into the tree and said,*
> *"Zacchaeus, hurry on down, for I am appointed to stay at your house today!"*
> *So he scurried down the tree and came face-to-face with Jesus.*
> *As Jesus left to go with Zacchaeus, many in the crowd complained, "Look at this!*
> *Of all the people to have dinner with, he's going to eat in the house of a crook."'*
> (Luke 19: 5-7 – TPT)

We notice three things about Jesus in these verses:

1. He saw Zacchaeus.
2. He knew Zacchaeus (He called him by name).
3. He called Zacchaeus (an invitation to a table).

Do we realise that Jesus sees us. He sees every fault, every failure, and every weakness. Even the things we try and hide, He sees. And yet for each of us, He calls us by name. It's an invitation to a Table to have communion with Him.

At this point in the story, Zacchaeus had not changed. He had not said a sinner's prayer, he had not filled in a decision card, he had not shown any signs of repentance. He was still the same greedy, selfish, lying, cheating, sinner that he had always been! But there was still an invitation to eat and drink with Jesus!

Do we see how foolish it is to think that we could ever be disqualified from the Lord's Table because of our behaviour? This was what the religious just could not get – He will truly eat with anyone who responds. And they don't have to change before they come. They can come to the table, just as they are.

And yet notice what happens next:

> 'But Zacchaeus stood up and said to the Lord, "Look, Lord! Here and now I give half of my possessions to the poor, and if I have cheated anybody out of anything, I will pay back four times the amount."' (v8)

At that table with Jesus something happened in the heart of Zacchaeus. Maybe it was a conviction of sin, maybe it was being overwhelmed by the love of the Christ (it was probably both), but this man was suddenly transformed.

Here is what those who preach an all-inclusive Jesus can sometimes miss. It is true that all are included at His Table. But don't miss the fact that at the Table, something changes within us. At the table we find a desire to change. At the table there is true repentance. At the Table grace empowers us to defeat sin. At the Table we are transformed from the inside out.

Sinners can come to the table, but they don't stay sinners! They become saints. Transformation doesn't have to come before the table, but it surely takes place at the Table!

At the table, face to face with Love Himself, you are moved and empowered to live differently.

> 'Jesus said to him, "Today salvation has come to this house, because this man, too, is a son of Abraham."' (v9)

Once again Jesus uses the word sozo to describe what Zacchaeus has experienced. He has been made whole, complete. What was broken had been put back to together again.

Abraham was of course the man whom God made covenant with and was the friend of God. Now at a table, God is revealing that this man too is a child of covenant, and a recipient of the blessing and favour of Heaven. He too has become a friend of God.

Perhaps from outside the house, these two men, one a notorious sinner and the other the Son of God could hear the grumbling and complaining of the religious over these two unlikely dining companions. But gradually the sound of laughter and conversation drowned them out as Zacchaeus began to relax in the presence of the One who is and always will be the friend of sinners. There is always room at His table for the hungry.

Perhaps the words of this old hymn sum it up the best:

> Just as I am, without one plea,
> But that Thy blood was shed for me,
> And that Thou bid'st me come to Thee,
> O Lamb of God, I come! I come!
>
> Just as I am, and waiting not
> To rid my soul of one dark blot;
> To Thee whose blood can cleanse each spot,
> O Lamb of God, I come, I come!
>
> Just as I am, though tossed about
> With many a conflict, many a doubt;
> Fightings within, and fears without,
> O Lamb of God, I come, I come!

Just as I am, poor, wretched, blind;
Sight, riches, healing of the mind;
Yes, all I need, in Thee to find,
O Lamb of God, I come, I come!

Just as I am, Thou wilt receive,
Wilt welcome, pardon, cleanse, relieve;
Because Thy promise I believe,
O Lamb of God, I come, I come!

Just as I am, Thy love unknown
Has broken every barrier down;
Now, to be Thine, yea, Thine alone,
O Lamb of God, I come, I come!

© Charlotte Elliott (1789-1871)

Prayer of Response

"Oh precious Jesus I come to you as a sinner. I have no confidence in my own righteousness but I have every confidence in your unconditional, overwhelming mercy. Who am I that I have been invited to Your table? You call me just as I am. I am a sinner, I am unclean, I am unworthy. But you welcome me, you accept me. I come just as I am. At Your Table I am made whole, at Your Table I am made complete. I receive your forgiveness. I receive your peace. Thank You Jesus that my debt has been cancelled. Thank You for Your gift of salvation. Oh Jesus thank You that You call me friend! Change me by Your grace and love. I repent of all sin. Let your Spirit so change me and transform me that I would truly never be the same again. Thank You Precious Lamb of God. My Saviour and my friend. Amen."

"The Eucharist is that love which surpasses all loves in heaven and on earth."

- *St. Bernard*

3

REMEMBRANCE - THE INVITATION INTO ENCOUNTER

"Do this in remembrance of Me."

(Luke 22:19)

The Communion Meal is a meal of remembrance. It is a time when we deliberately and pointedly look back two thousand years to Calvary, and to the suffering and death of our Lord.

As I am writing this chapter it is actually Passion Week, and many all over the world are focusing on the death and resurrection of Jesus. Even many who would not normally consider themselves religious may find thoughts of God entering their minds at this time of year.

The Apostle Paul writes in 1 Corinthians 11 about the "remembrance" aspect of the Lord's Table:

'For I received from the Lord what I also passed on to you: the Lord Jesus, on the night He was betrayed, took bread, and when He had given thanks, He broke it and said, "This is My body, which is for you; do this in remembrance of Me." In the same way, after supper He took the cup, saying, "This cup is the new covenant in My blood; do this, whenever you drink it, in remembrance of Me." For whenever

you eat this bread and drink this cup, you proclaim the Lord's death until He comes.'
(v23-26)

Twice in this passage is the word "remembrance" used. Jesus provided a way for us to always remember who He is and what He did 2,000 years ago on the cross.

Of course, for believers the cross should not be something that we occasionally think about but something that our whole lives revolve around. We should live, daily remembering what Christ did for us on the cross and walking in the reality of that love and grace. It is that sacrifice that should continually motivate us, overwhelm us, and transform us.

But does it? If we are honest as we go about our daily lives, going to work, paying bills, looking after children, and so forth, we can so easily find ourselves on the treadmill of life, barely having time to stop, look heavenward and remember.

But the Lord's Table ends that. The Lord's Table forces us to pause, stop, look back, and remember. In those moments at the Lord's Table, my focus is no longer on myself, my life, and my circumstances. Now my focus is on another place, another time, and another Person... Jerusalem, two thousand years ago, and "The Lamb of God who takes away the sins of the world."

The Power of Remembering

The word "remember" and the act of "remembrance" is important in the lives of God's people. God was and is always telling His people to remember.

Numerous times in the Old Testament God would repeat to His people, "I am the God of Abraham, Isaac and Jacob." In saying this He was trying to get them to remember who He was, the covenants He had made, and His faithfulness towards them and who they were, His covenant people.

In the book of Exodus God initiated the act of circumcision. Why? So that all Jewish men had a physical reminder that they were people of covenant.

Many times in the Old Testament God would remind His people of His great acts in their history. "Remember when you were slaves in Egypt and I delivered you?" "Remember when I defeated your enemies?" "Remember when I parted the Red Sea?"

He is constantly trying to get His people to look back and remember all that He has done for them and His faithfulness in the past.

What were the annual feasts and festivals that the Jews celebrated all about? Remembrance! Every Passover they reminded themselves of the lamb that was slain. Every Feast of Tabernacles they remembered their wilderness wanderings and God's promise to give them a permanent home.

In Deuteronomy 11 God told his people, 'Remember all the words that I have spoken to you,' and 'Don't forget them.' He even told them to tie His words as symbols on their hands and bind them on their foreheads so that they didn't forget.

In the book of Joshua, as His people were about to cross the Jordan to enter the promised land, God instructed them to place stones of memorial into the Jordan River; one for each tribe so that for generations to come, the Jews could remember all that God had done in delivering them.

One of the most beloved Psalms, Psalm 103, tells us to remind ourselves of all that

God has done for us:

> *'Praise the Lord, my soul; all my inmost being, praise His holy name. Praise the Lord, my soul, and forget not all His benefits – who forgives all your sins and heals all your diseases, who redeems your life from the pit and crowns you with love and compassion, who satisfies your desires with good things so that your youth is renewed like the eagles.' (v1-3)*

You are forgiven. You are healed. You are redeemed. You have been crowned. You have been satisfied. Remember these things. Don't ever forget!

The theme of remembrance is one that continues in the New Testament, especially in the writings of Peter. Writing to a church that was undergoing intense persecution, the theme of remembrance runs throughout his second epistle: 'So I will always remind you of these things, even though you know them and are firmly established in them.' (2 Peter 1:12) 'Dear friends this is now my second letter to you. I have written both of them as reminders to stimulate you to wholesome thinking. I want you to recall the words spoken in the past by the holy prophets.' (2 Peter 3:1-2)

Remember, remember, remember. Many times in Church we want a new revelation, a new prophetic word, new direction. Although God is the God of the "new thing" He is also the God who is constantly reminding us of what He has said and done in the past.

Peter wrote, 'Even though you know all this and are well established in it, I am going to remind you of what you already know. This is going to help stimulate you into wholesome thinking.'

Sometimes we don't need a new revelation or a new word, we just need to remind ourselves of what God has said and done in the past.

Ultimate Remembrance

Remembrance finds a truly special place of significance at the Lord's Table. It is there that Jesus is giving us a practical act - something tangible - in which we can always remember Him. "Whenever you meet together," do this, and remember. "Remember my Body. Remember my Blood."

Now I don't know about you but there are certain things in life that it's good not to forget. You should never forget your birthday. You should certainly never forget your spouse's birthday or your wedding anniversary! You should not forget where you put your car keys.

Why should you never forget these things? Because they are important.

There are certain key moments in my life that I don't think I will ever forget. I will never forget my wedding day. I will never forget when my children were born. Why not? Because they are moments of incredible importance and significance.

I am sure that we could all agree that the most important and significant moment in all of human history would be when Jesus died and rose again. Those three days changed everything, forever. So why would we need to be reminded? Why would Jesus give us a meal so that we would never forget Him? Surely we wouldn't anyway?

You don't need reminding of these key moments in your life, do you? In fact, it can be quite annoying if someone is constantly reminding you of what you already know. So why does God insist that we keep on reminding ourselves, every time we meet, of what we already know?
Because God knows human nature.
He knows that we do forget. He knows that we need continual reminding, even of

the most important thing He ever did for us.
Do you sometimes feel unloved? Do you sometimes feel lonely? Do you sometimes feel unworthy? Do you sometimes doubt that you are really forgiven?

We all do from time to time. Why? Because we have forgotten! We have forgotten that He loved us so much that He died for us. We have forgotten that He said He would always be with us. We have forgotten that He has made us righteous. We have forgotten that we are forgiven.

That is why He gives us the Bread and the Wine. To continually remind us of these things.

When do we get afraid? When we forget. When do we doubt? When we forget.

This is why we need the Lord's Table, and why we need it regularly. Because we have very bad memories when it comes to spiritual things!

We Are Not Alone

In this we are not alone. Take the disciples of Jesus as our example.

They had been sat with Jesus at the table when He had given them very clear instructions. "Whenever you meet together break bread, drink wine and remember." It couldn't be clearer!

But then, three days - get that, just three days later - where do we find them? They are together, but not around the Lord's Table, but hiding behind locked doors for fear of the Jewish leaders. (John 20:19)
How could they so quickly forget? They were gripped with fear and anxiety, they had

forgotten all of Jesus' instructions, given just three days before!

Jesus is so gracious. He walked into their prison of fear and gave them a powerful lesson in remembrance:

'On the evening of that first day of the week, when the disciples were together, with the doors locked for fear of the Jewish leaders, Jesus came and stood among them and said, "Peace be with you!" After He said this, He showed them His hands and side. The disciples were overjoyed when they saw the Lord.' (v19-20)

In showing them His hands and His side what was He doing? He was reminding them. He was effectively saying, "Have you forgotten already? Remember. Remember how much I love you. Remember that My blood was shed for you. Remember My body was broken for you. How quickly you forget. This is what I did for you. Why are you afraid? You are loved. You are redeemed. Don't ever forget."

Remember what I did. Remember who I am.

You would think that this time they would get the message. But just seven days later where do we find them? In the same house. Remembering Jesus? No, still with the doors locked. Still gripped in fear.

This time Thomas was with them:

'Now Thomas (also known as Didymus), one of the Twelve, was not with the disciples when Jesus came. So the other disciples told him, "We have seen the Lord!"'

But he said to them, "Unless I see the nail marks in his hands and put my finger where the nails were, and put my hand into his side, I will not believe."

A week later his disciples were in the house again, and Thomas was with them.'
(v24-26)

Thomas would forever be known as Doubting Thomas. But what was at the source of Thomas' doubts? A reluctance to believe that what Jesus had said was true. Jesus had told him that He would die and three days later rise again. It was this promise that Thomas doubted.

So when Jesus appears to Thomas, it is these doubts that He is addressing:

'Though the doors were locked, Jesus came and stood among them and said, "Peace be with you!" Then He said to Thomas, "Put your finger here; see My hands. Reach out your hand and put it into My side. Stop doubting and believe."' (v26-27)

What is Jesus saying? "Thomas remember. Look at my hands, look at my scars. Look and remember. Touch me, see that I am alive and remember. Didn't I say that I would die? Didn't I promise that I would rise again? I did it. I kept my promise. I always keep my promises. Don't ever forget that!"

It is easy to be critical of Thomas, but don't we do exactly the same? Don't we sometimes forget God's faithfulness? Don't we sometimes doubt if He really means what He has said? Don't we sometimes question His promises?

Like the other disciples don't we sometimes find ourselves in a prison of fear? A prison of shame? A prison of hopelessness?

What has happened? Quite simply we have forgotten. We have forgotten what Jesus did. We have forgotten who Jesus is. We have forgotten what Jesus has said.

Remembrance

Knowing this about us, Jesus gave us this remembrance meal. At the Lord's Table Jesus appears to us again and shows us His hands and side. He shows us the nail scars, the marks. He invites us to look, gaze, wonder, and search deeply into the mystery of His wounds. He invites us to see and He invites us to touch. He instructs us to stop. Stop doubting. Stop doubting, and believe. Stop and remember.

Remember what I have done:

I created you in my image, you are fearfully and wonderfully made. I have forgiven you. I have redeemed you. I have set you free. I have healed you. I have restored you. I have lifted you. I have made you righteous. I have given you My peace. I have given you My joy. I have given you eternal life.

Remember all of this. Don't ever forget. Remember.

Remember who I am:

Your Saviour. Your healer. Your redeemer. Your deliver. I am King of kings and Lord of lords. I am the Name above all Names. I am the conquering Lion of the tribe of Judah. I am faithful. I am the Light of the world. I am the Bright Morning Star. I am the Rock of Ages. I am the Good Shepherd. I am the Miracle Worker. I am the lover of your soul. I am your provider. I am the Alpha and the Omega.

Don't ever forget who I am. Remember.

Remember all that I have said:

I told you I love you. I told you that you are My friend. I told you that you are My child. I told you that I would never leave you. I told you that if you believe in Me you will never die. I told you that I am coming again. I told you that I have a plan for your life.

Don't doubt. I am faithful. I will always be faithful. I have always kept every promise and I always will.

You are a new creation. You are no longer condemned. You are His bride. You have His Spirit on the inside of you. You are blessed with every spiritual blessing. Greater is He that lives in you than he that is in the world.

Don't ever forget these things. Even though you know them, you need to be reminded. This is why He gave you a meal. To remember. So that you would never forget.

In the midst of your fears – remember. In the midst of your doubts – remember. In the midst of your confusion – remember. In the midst of your pain – remember. In the midst of loneliness – remember.

Remember that I have loved you with an everlasting love. Remember that I have forgiven you. Remember that I have brought you into My family and that all things are now yours. Remember that I am for you and not against you. Remember that I have overcome. Remember that you will never be alone, for surely I am with you always. Remember that in Me you have life. Remember that I am all that I say I am. Remember that my grace is always sufficient. Remember that I keep every promise and fulfil every word. Remember that joy always comes in the morning. Remember that death is always followed by resurrection.

The Remembrance Encounter

An act of remembrance is not unique to Christianity. Indeed, it is not just a religious concept. Why do people visit graveyards? To remember. Why do we sometimes have a moments silence at sporting events? We are remembering something or someone. Why do we have special days to remember those that have died in wars? We don't want to forget them or their sacrifice. Why do people take photographs? To remember.

But for the Christian, our act of remembrance is different and it is unique. For as the disciples gathered three days after the Crucifixion, Jesus not only came to remind them of the past but in doing so, something very special also took place:

'On the evening of that first day of the week, when the disciples were together, with the doors locked for fear of the Jewish leaders, Jesus came and stood among them and said, "Peace be with you!" After He said this, He showed them His hands and side. The disciples were overjoyed when they saw the Lord.

Again Jesus said, "Peace be with you! As the Father has sent me, I am sending you." And with that He breathed on them and said, 'Receive the Holy Spirit." (v19-22)

First, He shows them His hands and side, but then He breathes on them and says, "Receive My Spirit."

Simultaneously the disciples look back and remember the crucifixion, but then also receive the fresh infilling of the Spirit of God.

As they look back at their previous God encounters, they are propelled into a new God encounter, far greater than anything they had experienced before.

As He gently urges them to remember, they feel a gust of wind upon their faces. As they gaze on the wounds, as they remember the Passion of the Christ, the risen Saviour breathes upon them the Ruach of Heaven, His Holy Spirit. And the breath of His Spirit drives out doubt, drives out confusion, drives out fear. That moment of remembrance becomes a moment of divine exchange as the Spirit breathes into them His joy and peace.

This is why for the Christian the act of remembrance is different: The One we are remembering is alive! The One we are remembering is still with us. He is seated with us at the Table.

We don't have to rack our brains, and search our memory banks for something that happened so long ago that we can hardly remember. The Saviour is here. The Word is alive. His salvation is present. His blood still flows. It still speaks. The scars are still there.

He is still speaking. He is still showing us His hands and side. We can talk to Him. Gaze upon Him. He still invites us to reach out and touch Him.

His Spirit still moves at the Table. The wind of Heaven still blows upon our faces every time we turn and focus on Jesus.

And as we feel that sweet breath upon us, we are reminded all over again "This is real. He is alive. He is with me. I am communing with Him."

For the believer, every act of remembrance is an invitation into a fresh encounter with the One we are remembering.

He has given us more than a dead memorial stone, He has given us more than a story handed down from generation to generation. He has given us more than a mark in our bodies. He has given us living food, living drink, a living Saviour, a real, active, powerful Spirit.

He is saying, "Look back and remember, and then move forward and step into My reality."

Don't just remember what I have done, receive the fruit of all that I have done.

Receive My forgiveness, receive My healing, receive My freedom.

Don't just remember who I am – Encounter Me. Meet with Me. Commune with Me.

Don't just remind yourself of what I have said – Feed on My Word. Let My Words give you life. Let My promises sustain you. Let My Words become alive in you.

All that we can do in that moment is join with Thomas:

'Then the words spilled out of his heart–"You are my Lord, and you are my God!"'
(v28 – TPT)

God's Remembrance

We should remember in all of this that the remembrance meal is for our benefit and not for God's. After all, we are the ones who forget, God never does.

He knows us. He knows our name. He knows how many hairs are on our head. He knows our prayers and the deepest longings of our heart.

He has told us:

'Can a mother forget the baby at her breast and have no compassion on the child she has borne? Though she may forget, I will not forget you! See, I have engraved you on the palms of My hands; your walls are ever before Me.'
(Isaiah 49:15-16)

We don't need to constantly remind God of His promises and what He has said, like He somehow has a memory problem. After all, it is written:

'Not one of all the Lord's good promises to Israel failed; everyone was fulfilled.'
(Joshua 21:45)

Indeed there is only one thing that God has promised to forget:

'I, even I, am He who blots out your transgressions, for My own sake, and remembers your sins no more.' (Isaiah 43:25)

Now that is something that is worth remembering!

Prayer of Response

"Jesus, I choose today to stop, pause, and remember. I look back to all that You did on the Cross and I remember. I remember that You died for me. I remember that You shed your blood for me. Help me to never forget Your love for me. I remember Your goodness and Your faithfulness. I remember that You are for me and that You are with me. I remember that You keep all your promises. I remember that in You I am forgiven, free, healed and whole. I remember that I am a child of God.
Precious Holy Spirit, breathe on me. Holy Spirit, You are here with me right now.

I invite You to blow upon me and blow out all fear and all doubt. Breathe into me Your courage, Your boldness and Your peace. Holy Spirit as I receive You, I receive all that Jesus did for me on the cross. In You I receive and walk in the reality of Christ's finished work. Fill me Precious Holy Spirit. In the name of Jesus. Amen."

"Reverence, therefore, reverence this Table, of which we are all communicants. Christ, slain for us, the sacrificial victim who is placed thereon."

- *St. John of Chysostom*

4

REMEMBER - THE COVENANT

"This is My blood of the covenant, which is poured out for many for the forgiveness of sins."

(Matthew 26:28)

When Jesus was instituting the Lord's Table at His Last Supper, He used a powerful Biblical word: covenant. In the blood that He shed on the cross, He was making a new covenant between God and man – a covenant of grace. When we remember the Lord's death during Communion we are not only remembering the death that brought salvation but we are remembering the blood that enabled us to enter into covenant.

In order for us to fully understand the concept of covenant we are going to go on a journey that takes us back two thousand years before Christ, to a man that is still known today as the Father of Faith.

Abraham: The Father of Faith

In Genesis 15 God appears to Abram in a vision and gives him a powerful word that is both a declaration and a promise:

> *"Do not be afraid, Abram. I am your shield
> and your very great reward." (v1)*

During this encounter God promises the childless Abram that a son and heir will come from his own body (v4). Indeed, God's promise was so great that He declared that the descendants of Abram would be as numerous as the stars, (v5). God also promised Abram, the wanderer, that the land that he now stood would become his inheritance, (v7).

On receiving these incredible promises, the Bible says that Abram simply 'Believed the Lord,' (v6). It was the result of this powerful act of belief on Abram's part that enabled him to become known as the Father of Faith, (Romans 4:11). Four thousand years later Abram is still held up today as a wonderful example of a life of faith and trust in God.

It has been said that faith is the currency of heaven. When I travel overseas I have to use the currency of the land in order to purchase what I desire; even millions is useless if it's in the wrong currency.
Striving, the works of the flesh, self-effort – these won't enable you to receive anything from God. Only faith opens the windows of heaven and allows us to access all that God has available for us.

There is a wonderful Scripture in Hebrews 11 that links faith with the manifestation of God's blessings in our lives, 'by faith they gained what was promised,' (v33). It is one thing to have a promise, but it's another thing to actually gain or receive the promise.

All Christians have promises from God, but how many have received that promise and seen the manifestation in their lives?

In order for us to actually gain and receive and see the promises of God it will take faith, but more than that, a specific type of faith.

The Journey of Faith

As he believed God, the Bible says that the Lord credited righteousness to Abram, (v6). His actions of belief in the promises of God were enough for him to be declared righteous in the eyes of God. We might call this "saving faith". It is this type of faith that all Christians have – we have believed in Jesus and been made righteous.

However, despite believing in God and being declared righteous, Abram still had not received the manifestation of the promise of God. That would take place many years later as God took Abram on a journey of faith and trust. His initial acknowledgment of belief was simply the starting point in a life of faith.

So for us our initial belief in Christ is simply the start of our faith journey. We are called to grow and increase in faith, to go from one level of faith to the next, until we're walking in the kind of faith that truly takes hold of and receives the promises that God has given us.

Abram's faith grew and became so extraordinary that Romans 4 declares:

"Against all hope, Abraham in hope believed and so became the father of many nations, just as it had been said to him, "So shall your offspring be." Without weakening in his faith, he faced the fact that his body was as good as dead–since he was about a hundred years old–and that Sarah's womb was also dead. Yet he did not waver through unbelief regarding the promise of God, but was strengthened in his faith and gave glory to God, being fully persuaded that God had power to do what He had promised.' (v18-21)

Look again at some of the words and phrases used to describe the faith of Abram: without weakening, did not waver, and fully persuaded.

What an example of incredible, unshakeable faith! Yet it is interesting that the Bible says Abram was "strengthened in his faith." Although he had faith, something else happened that caused his faith to be strengthened and enabled him to become this giant of faith!

Following the verses that say that Abram believed God, Genesis 15 tells us that Abram asked a question of God, "O Sovereign Lord, how can I know that I will gain possession of it?"

Abram already believed God but now he wanted something to strengthen that faith, to allow his faith to reach the level where he could actually gain what he was believing for.

Many of us believe God can heal. Our question is, "God, how can I know that healing is for me?" Many of us believe God can provide. Our question is, "God, how can I know that you will provide for me?"

Belief is enough to save us. But it takes more than that to live in the fulfilment of promise. I too need my faith to be strengthened until I reach the point of knowing – knowing God will do what He has said, and knowing He will do it for me.

Do you know? Have you become fully persuaded? Are you convinced? This is Romans 4 kind of faith – the kind of faith that does not waver.

The Cutting of Covenant

In response to Abram's request for God to do something to strengthen his faith, God did something that would for us seem very strange.

> 'So the Lord said to him, "Bring me a heifer,
> a goat and a ram, each three years old,
> along with a dove and a young pigeon."
> Abram brought all these to Him, cut them in
> two and arranged the halves opposite each other;
> the birds, however, he did not cut in half.' (v9-10)

Although for us these verses seem bizarre, for Abram they were incredibly significant. God came down and partook in one of the customs of those days.

When two people wanted to guarantee that they would do what they had promised each other, they would enter into a covenant with each other. The greatest and most powerful of these covenants was a blood covenant.

When making a blood covenant, animals were sacrificed and then broken in two, and pieces of the dead animal laid either side of the pool of blood that had been created, and then each participant would walk in-between the pieces. This was known as the walk of blood.

In doing so, the two parties were entering into a blood covenant. This was a formal agreement of legal validity, one under a seal, with powerful consequences; a binding agreement, a contract, a solemn promise.

The ones making the covenant were declaring that if they ever broke it then the other party had the right to kill them. It was an irrevocable promise with unbreakable consequences.

> *'When the sun had set and darkness had fallen, a smoking fire pot with a blazing torch appeared and passed between the pieces. On that day the Lord made a covenant with Abram.' (Genesis 15:17-18)*

Here is God, the One who cannot lie, the One who cannot break His promises, the One who's Word shall never pass away, the One who cannot die – entering into a blood covenant with a man.

'Then the Lord said to him "know for certain…"' (v13). God was saying to Abram, "This is the sign that you can KNOW that I will do it. Abram, you don't just have a Word, you don't just have a Promise, you have a Blood Covenant.

Abram would leave this encounter forever changed – he was now a man with a covenant.

Remarkably, Abram didn't have a Bible to read, he didn't have access to teaching on faith, he didn't have a little book of Bible promises, but he had a covenant; and that was enough. He knew – this covenant has been sealed in blood, therefore it can never be broken!

This was how Abram knew that God would do it. This was why he did not waver. This was why he was fully persuaded. He had a covenant sealed in blood.

Even though circumstances were against him – he had a covenant. Even though time was against him – he had a covenant. Even though it was impossible in the natural – he had a covenant. Even though Sarah's womb was dead – he had a covenant. Even though he was over 100 years old – he had a covenant. Even though his body was as good as dead – he had a covenant.

The Bible tells us that Abram "faced the fact," yet he knew that the covenant that God had made with him was more powerful than the facts. "I don't know how God will do it, the facts are against me, but God has entered into a blood covenant – He must do what He has said He will do."

The result:

> *'And by faith even Sarah, who was past childbearing age, was enabled to bear children because she considered him faithful who had made the promise. And so from this one man, and he as good as dead, came descendants as numerous as the stars in the sky and as countless as the sand on the seashore.' (Hebrews 11:11-12)*

When Abram and Sarah saw the sacrifice that had been broken in two and the pool of blood – they knew that no matter how long it took, it had to come to pass, God must do what He had covenanted to do!

The Messiah's Covenant

Every Jew knew the story of Abraham, and the covenant God had made with him. They were a covenant nation, a covenant people. God kept the covenant he made to Abram. He is still keeping it today! Even though the Jewish people would forget God, He would never forget the covenant he made with them. Even though for the past four thousand years other nations have tried to annihilate the Jews, God has always been faithful to the covenant He made with Abram.

And so it is to people who understood the power and nature of a blood covenant, that Jesus would do this:

> *'After taking the cup, He gave thanks and said,*
> *"Take this and divide it among you. For I tell you*
> *I will not drink again from the fruit of the vine*
> *until the kingdom of God comes."*
>
> *And He took bread, gave thanks and broke it, and gave it to them, saying, "This is My body given*
> *for you; do this in remembrance of Me."*
>
> *In the same way, after the supper He took the*
> *cup, saying, "This cup is the new covenant*
> *in My blood, which is poured out for you."'*
> *(Luke 22:17-20)*

The breaking of the bread and the drinking of the cup were looking ahead to the breaking of His body and the shedding of His blood. And in itself this was looking back to that time with Abram, when the body of a sacrificed animal was broken in two, a pool of blood was created, and God entered into a blood covenant with man.

Here Jesus is saying, "I am entering into a new blood covenant. Not just with one man or one nation, but everyone who chooses to partake. This covenant will not be made with the blood of animals but with my very own blood."

This new covenant, surmised in Hebrews 8, is a covenant that allows all of us to have our sins forgiven and washed away. The new covenant enables us to be reconciled with God, and for all of us to know Him in a real and intimate way. The new covenant means that we no longer have to struggle or strive or obey laws and regulations in order to be made righteous, but Christ imputes His own righteousness and holiness into us, and then gives us His Spirit who will outwork the reality of that through us.

However, the New Covenant is more than that. Now all of us, Jew and Gentile are no longer separate but we are included as part of One New Man – we are in Christ. And in Christ we are recipients of "every Spiritual blessing," (Ephesians 1:3); we have received the full rights of sons (Galatians 4:6). Indeed, Paul says in 2 Corinthians 1 that now every promise God has made is "yes" in Christ, (v20).

Did you get that? No matter how many promises God has made – they are "yes" in Christ! That means that they are ours, they are available, they are accessible.

This means that healing is part of my covenant. Provision is part of my covenant. Freedom is part of my covenant. Peace and joy are part of my covenant. Answered prayer is part of my covenant. The blessing of God on my children is part of my covenant. Intimacy with the Holy Spirit is part of my covenant. Every word and every promise that God has spoken – I can now receive as part of my covenant rights.

Covenant People

The cross is more than just the forgiveness of sin and eternal life – it is God entering into a new covenant with man. A greater covenant. A better covenant. A covenant that encapsulates every other covenant and every other promise.

This is what Christ wants you to remember and know at The Table – He has entered into covenant with you. He has made an irrevocable promise, a binding legal contract sealed with His own blood, to promise you that He will do what He has said He will do.

Did God keep His promise to Abram? Yes! And if He kept the promise sealed with the blood of animals, how much more can we be certain that He will keep the covenant sealed in the blood of His Son?

This means that no matter what God has promised in His Word – we can be certain. We can be fully persuaded. We can know for sure. We have more than just a promise – we have a blood covenant.

Even if it seems impossible. Even if everything in the natural is against it happening. Even if you face the facts and they look contrary to the promise – the covenant is greater than the facts. You might not know how He will do it, or when He will do it – but He will do it. He cannot deny the covenant He has made.

One of the unique things about God's covenant with Abram was the one sided nature of it. Normally in a blood covenant both parties would agree to keep their side of the deal. But God, knowing man would never be faithful, took 100% responsibility in keeping the covenant. Three times in Genesis 15 God emphasised to Abram "I will" do all this. Unlike the later Mosaic covenant, this was a convent entirely of grace.

The Bible says that we are heirs of this covenant (Galatians 3). Jesus knows we cannot earn His promises through our good behaviour or striving, and so He made His covenant one of pure grace, "I will do all this. All you have to do is believe and receive".

Remembrance

God has made the covenant and God will keep the covenant. Our part is to remember the covenant!

In Luke 13, Jesus encounters a woman in a synagogue who for eighteen years had been crippled by a spirit of infirmity. It seems that no one was particularly concerned about this, and indeed after Jesus heals and restores her, they even argue that Jesus had broken the law by healing on a Sabbath. Imagine that! They would rather her remain bound than be healed if it meant breaking their interpretation of the Mosaic Law.

But Jesus, following on from giving an illustration, about loosing a tied up animal even if it was on a Sabbath, makes a powerful statement. He takes them back to a covenant that was made long before the Mosaic covenant, "Should not this woman, a daughter of Abraham, whom Satan has kept bound for eighteen long years, be set free on the Sabbath day from what bound her?"

He is inviting them to remember. Remember the covenant God made all those years ago. They had become so preoccupied with keeping their religious laws and duties that they had forgotten that they were covenant people. This woman was a daughter of covenant. Satan had no right to bind her and they had no right to deny her her miracle. She had covenant rights.

I wonder if sometimes we go through life, bound and bent over, forgetting just who we are, what He has said, and what He has done. Communion is not just a reminder of what Jesus did, but it is a reminder of who we are and what we have in Him.

Every time we take communion we are reminding ourselves, "I am a child of covenant," and "I have covenantal rights."

The act of remembrance is not for God's benefit – He never forgets. We are the ones who forget.

Although God's covenant with Abram was unconditional, in Genesis 17, God instituted the act of circumcision. Circumcision was a physical act of remembrance of the spiritual reality of the covenant. They were receiving something in their body, in their flesh, to remind them of the covenant that God had made. This was so important that God said that anyone who didn't circumcise their flesh would be cut off from God's people, (v14).

God was not saying that circumcision itself saved them. The covenant had already been made, it was established, it was unconditional, it was eternal. What God was saying was, if you want to be a partaker of this covenant, you now have to receive the sign of covenant in your body.

I hope the parallel is obvious. Christ's covenant is finished, it's done and it's a covenant of grace. We can't earn or work for it. However we must now receive the sign of His covenant into our body – the Bread and the Wine. These in themselves have no power to save us, just as circumcision has no power to save the Jews, but in receiving the Bread and Wine into our physical bodies we are partaking of the body and blood of Christ, and entering into the reality of all that Christ has already purchased for us.

Never Forget

So Communion for us is an act of remembrance, but just what are we remembering? We are remembering that we are covenant people! We are remembering that all of God's promises for our lives are based on a covenant sealed with His own blood. On the days when my guilt and shame are overwhelming, I take communion and remind myself, "I am forgiven, I am righteous, I am a new creation." On the days when I am sick, I take communion and I remind myself, "By His stripes I am healed." On the days when I am in the midst of a battle, I take communion and I remind myself, "He is good. He is my peace. He is my joy. He is my comfort. He is a faithful God and He will do what He has said He will do!"

However, communion is more than just reminding myself of His covenant. It is receiving in my flesh the signs of the covenant, and in doing so entering into the reality and manifestation of the covenant itself.

I will conclude this chapter with this powerful true story:

Adoniram Judson was a remarkable missionary to Burma, remarkable not in the least because he seemed to have no success, no converts for well over a decade, yet he stuck to it. Indeed the tribes he was ministering to had become impatient and hostile towards him. There came a day of confrontation when the chief of one tribe had tied Judson up and was about to throw him to the flames. He came and eyeballed Judson and said, "What do you think now of your God, now that you are about to die?" Judson stared right back at him and said these memorable words, "My future is as bright as the promises of God." Famously, it was the tribal chief who blinked, untied Judson and said he would hear more of this God. This was the day Christianity took root in Burma.

Be encouraged. We are covenant people! Our hope is built on nothing less than the Word of God, with His Anointed One as the anchor of our souls. In Him our future is bright, indeed glorious!

Prayer of Response

"Father, thank you that I am your child and that I am a child of covenant. Thank you that I have a covenant sealed in the blood of Your Son. You will be faithful to keep Your covenant because you are a faithful, covenant keeping God. You will do all that

You have covenanted to do. Satan has no right to steal, kill or destroy in my life because I have covenant rights. The covenant You have made entitles me to healing, to answered prayer and access to Your throne room. Every blessing is mine. You have promised to provide for me. I will be blessed, my home shall be blessed, my marriage shall be blessed, my children shall be blessed. You are faithful and will keep Your promises. As I receive the Bread and the Wine, I both remember and thank You for the covenant that you have made and I receive all of Your promises, saying "amen" to all that You have already said "yes" to in Christ. Thank you Father. In the name of Jesus. Amen."

"Just as by melting two candles together you get one piece of wax, so I think, one who receives the flesh and blood of Jesus is fused together with Him, and the soul finds that He is in Christ and Christ is in him."

- St. Cyril of Jerusalem

5

THE COMMUNION ENCOUNTER
(PART ONE)

"Then the two told what had happened on the way, and how Jesus was recognised by them when He broke the bread.

(Luke 24:35)

So far in this book we have looked at the great longing that God has for communion with His children. This is the significance of the Table, it is one of the methods that God uses to have fellowship with us which is what He longs for more than anything else. We have also looked at the truth that Communion is for us an act of remembrance. Whenever we come to the Lord's Table we are looking back two thousand years to the death and resurrection of Jesus on the cross. For us this act of remembrance should be a powerful and important moment in our lives, and on a regular basis. In the midst of the trials and circumstances of our lives, and our own struggle with sin, how often we forget the basic truths – I am loved, I am forgiven, I am a child of covenant. Communion helps us focus. Helps us remember.

However, I would suggest that the Lord's Table has to be about so much more than just remembering the Cross. It has to be about so much more than just looking back to what happened at Calvary. The Christian act of remembrance is more than just remembering a historical event - it is the invitation into a fresh, present day encounter.

Having been in countless Communion services during my life I can confidently say that the overwhelming majority of them have been focused entirely on the act of remembrance. Here is a typical of the Communion service: the bread and wine placed on a table in which is engrained the words, "This do in remembrance of me." The person leading Communion then says a few words such as, "As we come to the Lord's Table we are reminding ourselves of what Jesus did for us on the Cross." Then commonly, the praise team will sing a song about the Cross, or perhaps the love of God.

It seems like the whole act of coming to the Lord's Table has been reduced down to only being seen as an act of remembrance. I wonder if sometimes that is why Communion can be a dull and dare I say it, boring part of our worship experience. We try and remind ourselves of the wonder of the Cross, but these are words and scriptures we have heard countless times before. This week's "Communion Song" contains similar sentiments to the one that we sang the week before. It's the same old tired prayers of thanksgiving from the same people each week. No wonder some churches no longer partake of Communion regularly. There are only so many times you can talk about the same things without it sounding and becoming stale.

But what if the Lord's Table was about more than just looking back and remembering? What if in making the Lord's Table only about remembrance, we are missing the act of communion itself.

Of course, Communion is not just about looking back, it's also about looking forward. We are remembering the promise of Jesus that He will come again and take us to the future Table and the Wedding Supper of the Lamb. However, in the looking forward, we can still miss the "now." We still miss the communion that is in the Communion.

The Lord's Table is remembering the past and longing for the future. But it is also an experience, an encounter in the now. The Master is here with us at the Table. He is here inviting us not just to remember, but to dine, to commune, to fellowship. This is the beating heart of this book - to put the communion back in the Communion.

Experiencing Him in Communion

Luke 24 and the story of the two men on the Road to Emmaus is a powerful example of what can take place when we encounter Him at The Table.

> 'Now that same day two of them were going to a village called Emmaus, about seven miles from Jerusalem. They were talking with each other about everything that had happened. As they talked and discussed these things with each other, Jesus Himself came up and walked along with them; but they were kept from recognizing Him.
>
> He asked them, "What are you discussing together as you walk along?" They stood still, their faces downcast. One of them, named Cleopas, asked Him, "Are you the only one visiting Jerusalem who does not know the things that have happened there in these days?"
> "What things?" He asked.
> "About Jesus of Nazareth," they replied. "He was a prophet, powerful in word and deed before God and all the people. The chief priests and our rulers handed him over to be sentenced to death, and they crucified him; but we had hoped that he was the one who was going to redeem Israel. And what is more, it is the third day since all this took place. In addition, some of our women amazed us. They went to the tomb early this morning but didn't find his body. They came and told us that they had seen a vision of angels, who said he was alive. Then some of our companions went to the tomb and found it just as the women had said, but they did not see Jesus."

He said to them, "How foolish you are, and how slow to believe all that the prophets have spoken! Did not the Messiah have to suffer these things and then enter His glory?" And beginning with Moses and all the Prophets, He explained to them what was said in all the Scriptures concerning Himself.

As they approached the village to which they were going, Jesus continued on as if He were going farther. But they urged him strongly, "Stay with us, for it is nearly evening; the day is almost over." So He went in to stay with them.

When He was at the table with them, He took bread, gave thanks, broke it and began to give it to them. Then their eyes were opened and they recognized Him, and He disappeared from their sight. They asked each other, "Were not our hearts burning within us while He talked with us on the road and opened the Scriptures to us?" (Luke 24:13-32)

What were these two men doing as they were walking on the Emmaus Road that day? They were remembering. They were looking back to the crucifixion and death of Jesus. When they encountered the mysterious third man they continued this act of remembrance, going over once again the story of the death of the Nazarene.

But surprisingly, this act of remembrance was doing them little good. They were downcast, discouraged and disappointed. They were looking back with nostalgia and wondering where it had all gone wrong. There was little hope or joy in their present and certainly not in their future.

They didn't realise that they were in the presence of the very One who they were remembering. Little did they realise that they had an opportunity to fellowship, commune with and encounter the One who had not only died, but who was alive, and was with them!

They should have realised as He spoke with them and their hearts were ignited by the fire of heaven, that they were receiving more than a Bible study on the road that day, they were conversing with the very Word of God Himself. His life giving and life creating words were piercing their dullness and setting their hearts on fire.

'When He was at the table with them,' (v30). Oh, the power of these words! This act of the breaking of bread was more than just an act of remembrance, it was more than just looking back. He was there at the table with them as they broke bread! Their Saviour was there! They were fellowshipping with God Himself at the table!

Just looking back and remembering, whilst having some benefits has in itself no power to change us. Only a fresh, new encounter with the Living God will do that. When our Communion services go from just reminding each other of the old story, and we come to realise that He is actually here with us at the table – get ready for our acts of Communion to be life changing and transforming!

> *'He took bread, gave thanks, broke it and began to give it to them. Then their eyes were opened and they recognised Him.' (v30-31)*

Although He was there all the time, it was during the breaking of bread that they "recognised Him." The Greek word used here for "recognised" is the word Ginosko; it means to come to know, to experience. It doesn't mean to just intellectually know something, but to know something by experience or exposure. This same word can also be used for the act of sexual intimacy between married couples.

How wonderful this is! Although Jesus is always with us, something wonderful happens as I break bread with Him at the table. It is during the act of communion with Him at the Table that I experience Him, and have an encounter with Him. It is at the Table that I am exposed to His presence. As I recognise that He is here with me, I am no longer just remembering with my mind the past but my whole being – spirit, soul and body is experiencing Him in the now. It is here at the Table, that I am experiencing true intimacy with the Bridegroom.

This is where transformation takes place. 'Their eyes were opened,' (v31) it was like the veil that was covering their senses, making them blind and dull to the reality of His presence was suddenly lifted as they broke bread with Him.

Paul said it like this in 2 Corinthians 3:

'But whenever anyone turns to the Lord, the veil is taken away. Now the Lord is the Spirit, and where the Spirit of the Lord is, there is freedom. And we all, who with unveiled faces contemplate the Lord's glory, are being transformed into His image with ever-increasing glory, which comes from the Lord, who is the Spirit.' (v16-18)

At the Lord's Table we deliberately turn our thoughts, attention, worship, and gaze upon Jesus. It is in that moment that the veils that keep us dull, discouraged and spiritually blind are lifted. It is at the Table, as we behold the Lamb that we see Him face to face. In this powerful act of communion we experience true freedom, and we ourselves are transformed as we become like the One we behold.

Whilst the NIV translation says that they "recognised Him," the NKJV says "they knew Him." There is such beauty in this translation! It is here, at the Table that we truly come to know Him. We can never fully know Him just by reminding ourselves of what happened two thousand years ago; but in actually communing with Him at the Table is how we truly get to know Him, not just as an historical figure, but as a present day lover and friend.

Staying with the NKJV for a moment - as they came to know Him - this translation says, "they rose up that very hour and returned to Jerusalem." (v33) When we truly encounter Him at the Table it demands a response to arise. We rise up from our discouragement. We rise up out of our despair and disappointment. We rise up and enter into joy and hope. We return to our Jerusalem, the place which speaks of our future destiny, purpose, and future infillings.

Can you imagine the journey back to Jerusalem and how different it was? Can you imagine the joy, excitement, and eagerness to share what had just happened with others? Why? They had had an encounter with Jesus as they broke bread! When was the last time you left a Communion service like that?

What Has Gone Wrong?

So how did we get from the Lord's Table being a powerful moment of encounter to what has become, for many, something dull and overly familiar?

At the start of every chapter in this book, there is a quote from one of the Church Fathers/Mothers, or one of the ancient Christian mystics. These old men and women of God, some writing over a thousand years ago, predate Martin Luther and his protestant reformation by hundreds of years.

Whilst I do not believe every point of doctrine from the likes of Augustine and his contemporaries, there is no doubt that these Fathers and Mothers of the Church encountered God at the Table in powerful ways, like many never have in our modern Communion services.

The ancients of the Church believed powerfully in the act of Communion. For them, the Lord's Table was the high point of peoples worship experience. It was at the Table that they met with the risen Jesus, and ate and drank of His presence. They truly believed that Jesus was in the Communion, that the Holy Spirit was present in the Bread and the Wine.

Like with any truth, religion has a habit of perverting and distorting things, and this became true of Communion. False teaching crept in that during Communion, the Bread and the Wine literally became the flesh and blood of Jesus Christ. It was then taught that the Bread and the Wine could in themselves bring salvation. People began to live like the devil during the week, but then in receiving the flesh and blood of Christ, they believed they were receiving salvation.

500 hundred years ago, Martin Luther nailed his 95 theses to the door of the Wittenberg Castle Church, and so began the Protestant Reformation and the breaking away of the Catholic Church, which had become corrupt and full of heresy and idolatry. One of the heresies that the Protestant Reformation began to correct was the heresy surrounding Communion. Protestantism began to rightly teach that the Bread and Wine did not literally become the flesh and blood of Jesus and that there was no power in taking Communion to save anyone - only faith in Christ can do that. And so Communion became - not an act of salvation, but - a remembrance of salvation. A looking back to where our salvation really took place, not in a religious act, but on a cross two thousand years ago. Today, for the vast majority of Protestants, this is what Communion represents, an act of remembrance.

But I wonder if in rightly breaking away from some of the heresy's that the Catholic Church had allowed to creep in, if the pendulum has now swung too far the other way. While for 500 hundred years Communion has been seen primarily as an act of remembrance, we would do well to remember that for 1,500 years Communion was seen as so much more than that!

I wonder if we are sometimes so afraid of leading people into the error of transubstantiation that we continually refer to the Bread and the Wine as just "emblems," and in doing so do them a great disservice.

I do not believe that the Bread and the Wine literally become the body and blood of Jesus. But I do believe that there is "presence" there; they are more than just symbols, more than just religious tokens.

The Communion Revival

As an evangelist the vast majority of my meetings conclude with an altar call, or ministry time. It is here I encourage sinners and backsliders to come to the altar, and receive forgiveness and salvation. It is here that I will encourage the sick and bound to come, and receive healing and freedom. These altar/ministry times are powerful and I have countless testimonies of people encountering God at the altar. Sometimes my whole message is taking people on a journey with the destination of the altar, where they can meet with God. For some churches, the altar call or ministry time is the main moment where people come and have their God encounter.

Would it surprise you to learn that the altar call is a relatively new concept in Christendom? It was really only during the ministry of the great Charles Finney (1792-1875) that the cry "O, come to the altar," became the main focus of the churches evangelistic efforts. The popularity of coming to a ministry time is an even more recent phenomenon.

For the vast majority of the past two thousand years, the appeal of the Church was not "Come to the altar," but was "Come to the Table." Do you need forgiveness? - come to the Table. Do you need healing? - come to the Table. Do you long to meet with God? - come to the Table! It was here, at the Table that people had God encounters.

I am grateful of the writings of J. Todd Billings in his book Remembrance, Communion and Hope for the research that he has undertaken into the Holy Fairs that were held in the Scottish Reformed churches from the 1620's until the late eighteenth and early nineteenth century. Holy Fairs were large festivals, four to five days in length, culminating in the celebration of Communion. Prior to the act of Communion itself, all the teaching, preaching and singing were building up to and preparing people for the time when they would come to the Table. People were encouraged to fast and prepare their hearts for that moment. They were taught that Jesus was present at the Table through the Holy Spirit and that as they ate and drank they would experience a presence that was real, powerful and overwhelming.

Billings describes how on the day of Communion itself that "participants wore their finest clothes and the celebration took place at long tables covered with clean, white linens. Each had a place at Christ's Table. Rich and poor, male and female, celebrated together - no one was to receive superior or inferior wine and bread. Psalms and hymns were sung; tears of joy were shed at the table. Some fainted in their excitement; all celebrated. These gatherings deeply engaged the affections and the senses, as they centred on a message of passionate communion with Christ by the Spirit's power."

It was at the Table of the Lord at these Holy Fairs that people would weep, faint, groan, tremble, be filled with holy laughter, and experience spiritual revival. Now compare that with the last Communion service you had!

A couple of years ago I had the privilege of visiting the site of the Cane Ridge revival, held in Kentucky in 1801. It became the largest and most famous hub of revival that happened in the Second Great Awakening. What is interesting was that these revival services were focused on the act of Communion.

The revival began during what was known as "communions," a version of the Scottish reformed Holy Fairs. Lasting three to five days, the singing, preaching, and teaching would centre around the Lord's Table, culminating in the act of Communion itself. Interestingly, the most popular texts for the preachers were not the gospel accounts of the crucifixion but the ancient writings of the Song of Songs. Coming to the Table was seen not just as an act of remembering a crucified Saviour, but an act of intimate communion with a loving Bridegroom.

Some 20,000 people would gather at these revival services as the preacher would seek to woo the people to the Table, preaching on the "Ravishing Beauty and Glory of Christ," and inviting them to "Sit under the Shadow of this blessed Apple Tree, and taste His pleasant fruits."

One of the pioneers of that revival, James McGready, would often exhort listeners to feast at Christ's Table on the hidden manna and be refreshed with the new wine of Canaan. McGready would say the following:

"The real Christian, the new born child of God, loves to see Jesus and behold His glory, and with joy, delight, and wonder to admire and adore His soul attracting beauty and loveliness; and for this reason - He is the centre of his love, his portion, his inheritance, and the soul and substance of his happiness. His greatest happiness on earth is to 'see Jesus' - to have sweet communion with him, and to feel His love shed abroad in his heart. The sacrament of the Supper is one of the most affecting institutions of Heaven, and one of the nearest approaches to God that can be made on this side of eternity, in which believers are permitted to hold intimate conversation with our blessed Jesus."

During these revival services, men and women would have incredible encounters with God at the Table. One communicant said of their experience, "When I came to the Lord's Table, He was pleased to give me much of His gracious presence, and I may say that He took me into His banqueting house, and His banner over me was love."

Another communicant said that as they made their way to the Table, "I could scarce walk, I was swallowed up in love and enflamed affection for the Redeemer."

Yet another communicant, who had been filled with grief at the death of her husband, and left alone with seven children, had in her words a "kind of visit of heaven" where she "heard the voice of my Beloved, 'behold He cometh - skipping over the mountains and leaping over the hills.' I was so much ravished by His love, that I scarce knew where I was."

During these times of Communion - of being wooed to the Table - observers described multitudes being swept down in a moment as if a battery of a thousand guns had been opened upon them. This was followed by shrieks and shouts. Some lay motionless for hours, others cried out as if in torment, seeking peace. Some laughed uncontrollably and hysterically and others jerked back and forth.

These phenomenon sound like something you would witness at an extreme Charismatic revival service where an evangelist is laying hands on people at an altar and people are lined up with catchers behind them.

But these remarkable incidents took place as people were eating bread and drinking wine at the Lord's Table. This was not an advertised revival service but a Communion service.

The Response?

In reading of these old moves of God I am deeply challenged. I love altar calls and ministry times, and I firmly believe that they have a vital role to play in people's walk with God. But in our focus on the altar, have we neglected the Table? What if we once again started to call people back to the Table to meet with God? What if the Lord's Supper was once again the high point of people's spiritual experience? What if our most powerful God moments and God encounters were found in having communion during Communion? Is the Lord's Table an ancient well of encounter that needs to be re-dug? What would happen if in our church gatherings we began to tap into this powerful source of intimacy with our Bridegroom?

A Prayer of Response

"Precious Jesus, as I sit at the Table I recognise that You are sat here with me. I am in the presence of the Living God. Jesus open my eyes. I want to see You. I want to know You. My heart longs for intimacy with You. Precious Jesus, fill my whole being, spirit, soul, and body with Your glorious Presence. I gaze upon You and in doing so I receive Your peace, Your joy, and Your freedom. Heal me and make me whole. Let me experience the true depths of Your love. Amen."

"To partake of the Holy body and blood of Christ is good and beneficial, for He says quite plainly: he that eats My flesh and drinks My blood has eternal life. Who can doubt that to share continually in life is the same thing as having life abundantly."

- St. Basil the Great

6

THE COMMUNION ENCOUNTER
(PART TWO)

"It is good for our hearts to be strengthened by grace, not by eating ceremonial foods, which is of no benefit to those who do so. We have an altar from which those who minister at the tabernacle have no right to eat."

(Hebrews 13:9-10)

It was this verse in Hebrews that first began to challenge my thinking about the way that we approach the Lord's Table and the act of Communion. After years of sitting in Communion services around the world I had become concerned that even in more contemporary, Spirit-filled churches, Communion had become ceremonial, religious, and routine. The Bread and the Wine had become just symbols, often dismissed even as they were being partaken of as "just the emblems."

But here the writer of Hebrews compares two meals and two covenants. The Old Covenant, represented by the Tabernacle of Moses contained just ceremonial food (perhaps speaking of the bread that was placed on the altar in the Holy Place). Overtime this bread, which the Old Testament refers to as "the bread of the Presence" (Exodus 25:30) had become just an empty religious emblem. Hebrews tells us that just eating this bread as an emblem, as part of a religious ceremony has "no benefit" for those who eat of it.

But then the writer contrasts this bread with the bread of the New Covenant - an altar from which those before Christ could not eat of - but we can. The writer is indicating that the bread that we eat is not just ceremonial, not just an emblem, but something that is of benefit to us as we partake.

The challenge is that if we only see the Bread and Wine as tokens, we can eat and drink, and it may be nice, but it doesn't actually do us any good. But if we see that the Bread and Wine are so much more than that, eating and drinking it becomes of great benefit to us.

It is as we eat and drink of the bread and wine of the New Covenant that our "hearts are strengthened by grace." This is powerful! As we come to the Lord's Table we are not just partaking of religious symbols but we are feeding on grace itself! We are being nourished, sustained and empowered by grace!

Hebrews says that this is good for our hearts! The word "good" here can also be translated "beautiful" - it is a beautiful thing to be strengthened by grace which comes through eating and drinking at the Lord's Table. The Passion Translation says: "It is more beautiful to feast on grace and be inwardly strengthened."

The Lord's Table is spiritual nourishment for my body, soul, and spirit. As I partake I am being strengthened in my inner man (my spirit), renewed in my soul, and my physical body is being quickened by the resurrection life.

> *'He that eats my body and drinks my blood*
> *is strengthened in me and I in him.'*
> *(Aramaic translation of John 6:56)*

Spiritual Nourishment

In 1 Kings 19, the prophet Elijah is in a very low place both physically, emotionally, and spiritually. After the great high of Mount Carmel, Elijah is now burnt out, and ready to quit. The words of Jezebel have acted like a poison of fear that have paralysed him. He is in such a state of depression that he is even wishing for his life to be over.

God's remedy for his suicidal prophets' depression is heavenly food:

'An angel touched him and said, "Get up and eat." He looked around, and there by his head was some bread baked over hot coals, and a jar of water. He ate and drank and then lay down again. The angel of the Lord came back a second time and touched him and said, "Get up and eat, for the journey is too much for you." So he got up and ate and drank. Strengthened by that food, he travelled for forty days and forty nights until he reached Horeb, the mountain of God.' (v5-8)

Although there is no indication from where this food came from, the fact that it was delivered by an angel indicates that it didn't come from Elijah's local supermarket! This was supernatural food that would strengthen and empower him for the next 40 days and nights.

Depression, anxiety, fear, and weariness; even thoughts of suicide can effect even great men and women of God. God's answer is the same as it was to Elijah - get up and eat. The Bread and Wine at my Table will sustain, empower and strengthen you.

John Calvin put it like this: 'Now Christ is the only food of our soul, and therefore our Heavenly Father invites us to Christ, that, refreshed by partaking of Him, we may repeatedly gather strength.'

Psalm 104:15 talks of 'Bread that sustains his (man's) heart.' How often should we partake of Communion? If it is only an act of remembrance then I guess doing it too often can become routine. But if the Table is spiritual nourishment, the thing that actually sustains us, what then? How often do our bodies need nourishment? Three meals a day? Then how much more our spirits?

Psalm 78:19 tells us that God is a God who prepares a table in the wilderness for His children. The children of Israel called the bread that came from heaven "manna" - what is it? They didn't know what they were eating, they didn't know the source. They didn't realise that they were actually eating the bread of angels!

> *'Still He spoke on their behalf and the skies opened up; the windows of heaven poured out food, the mercy bread-manna. The grain of grace fell from the clouds. Humans ate angels' food–the meal of the mighty ones. His grace gave them more than enough!'*
> *(v24-25 - TPT)*

They were unaware that they were not eating ordinary bread - they were eating the bread of angels - something heavenly, and supernatural. They were feeding on food from another dimension.

This world in which we live can often feel like a wilderness. The world often feels barren and empty. Yet on this sojourn as we wait to enter our Heavenly Canaan, we can be encouraged that there is a Table prepared for all of us in the wilderness.

This table contains more than just ordinary bread. We are eating something divine, supernatural, of another world. The Bible tells us that as they were drinking in the wilderness it was Christ that they were drinking of (1 Corinthians 10:4). Yet what they had was just the prophetic foreshadowing. The reality is available for us. We truly eat and drink of Christ in Communion.

Interestingly in Hebrew the word for "take a drink" and the word for "kiss" are nearly the same, thereby indicating the act of drinking the cup is in itself an act of intimacy.

Andrew Murray (1828-1917) said "The blood of Jesus is my drink of life. Jesus' love is the power of my life. How powerful, how heavenly must that life be which is nourished by the new wine of the Kingdom and has communion with the blood of God's Son, not only by cleansing, but also by drinking"

Union With Christ

The early church fathers firmly believed that as they took Communion something supernatural, and Heavenly took place. This is in contrast with the modern day Protestant thinking that the Bread and Wine are merely symbolic emblems. As I have already covered, I do not believe in the doctrine of Transubstantiation - that the Bread and Wine are literally the body and blood of Jesus. But I also do not believe either that the Bread and Wine are just empty symbols.

J. Todd Billings in his book Remembrance, Communion and Hope argues that although the Bread and Wine are not to be adored in themselves, they are nevertheless "instruments" of the Spirit that "exhibit and offer Christ." Billings states that the Lord's Table doesn't just offer empty signs, but at the Supper 'believers feed upon Christ Himself by the Spirit.' Although Jesus Christ Himself is the substance (not the Bread and Wine), He has so closely identified Himself with the Bread and Wine, that they are never just empty symbols, but one of the methods that the Holy Spirit uses to allow us to feed on Christ Himself.

Perhaps another way of looking at this that may be particularly helpful for Pentecostal/

Charismatic readers is to think of the laying on of hands during a healing service. The person that is sick will approach the minister, who will lay hands on the person requiring ministry. Now whose hands are being laid on? Do we believe that the hands of the minister have literally become the hands of Jesus? No of course not. But do we believe that the laying on of hands is just an empty, symbolic gesture? No, we don't believe that either. The hands remain the hands of the person praying, but nevertheless in that moment, they are infused by the Spirit, and in faith they become the hands of Jesus and received in faith - they become a source of healing.

Likewise, the Bread and Wine never literally become the body and blood of Christ, but neither are they empty religious symbols. If we approach in faith, the Bread and Wine become infused with the presence of Christ and as we receive in faith, they become for us His flesh and His blood; instruments of His divine power, love and mercy.

Paul puts it like this in 1 Corinthians:

'When we drink the cup of blessing, aren't we taking into ourselves the blood, the very life, of Christ? And isn't it the same with the loaf of bread we break and eat? Don't we take into ourselves the body, the very life, of Christ?' (10:16 - The Mess)

Paul firmly believed that as he ate the bread and drank the wine at the Table, he was receiving - taking into himself - the very life of Christ. The NIV says that as we eat the bread and drink the cup we are participating in the body and blood of Christ. The Greek word for "participate" that is used here is the word koinonia; it means fellowship, sharing, intimacy.

Paul taught very clearly that the Lord's Table is not just where we reflect from a distance, but the place we go, to truly enter into a deep place of communion and intimacy with Christ.

Again I repeat, if the Lord's Table is only a thinking back to the Cross, we have diluted its power and impact. There is meant to be a deep union with Christ that takes place at the Table.

'In communion at the Supper, the Lord Jesus offers His own person, His very presence, to His people, those who are hopelessly incomplete without Him.'
J. Todd Billings

'The purpose of the Lord's Supper is to receive from Christ the nourishment and strength and hope and joy that come from feasting our souls on all that He purchased for us on the Cross, especially His own fellowship.'
John Piper

Real Food and Real Drink

John 6 contains one of Jesus' most controversial sermons. It was controversial when He said it, leading to a large group of His disciples turning their backs on Him (v66) and it also a little contentious today.

It is in John 6 that Jesus tells His disciples that they must eat His flesh and drink His blood, even stating that unless you eat His flesh and drink His blood "you have no life in you."

What was Jesus referring to when He said these words? I am sure we can all agree that He was not promoting cannibalism! He was speaking of a spiritual reality. When he uses the words, eat, drink, flesh, and blood our minds are immediately drawn to the Last Supper and the Lord's Table. So some preachers teach that this is what Jesus is referring to - that John 6 is speaking of the Communion Table.

Others will argue that John 6 took place long before the Last Supper and therefore has nothing to do with the Communion Table at all, and that He is speaking not of the Breaking of Bread, but of our spiritual union with Him.

The truth is somewhere in-between. It would be wrong to say that John 6 is exclusive teaching on the Lord's Table, but the language used is so clear that it would be wrong to say that this teaching has nothing to do with the Breaking of Bread at all. John 6 is speaking of our spiritual union with Christ, but an important part of that union is dining with Him at the Table. The physical act of eating the bread and drinking the wine is part of our spiritual communion - eating of Him, drinking of Him.

> *'Jesus said to them, "Very truly I tell you, it is not Moses who has given you the bread from Heaven, but it is my Father who gives you the true bread from Heaven. For the bread of God is the bread that comes down from heaven and gives life to the world."' (v32-33)*

> *'Then Jesus declared, 'I am the bread of life. Whoever comes to Me will never go hungry, and whoever believes in Me will never be thirsty.' (v35)*

Jesus is the Bread of God. The bread - the thing we feed on, that sustains us as we eat at the Table - is His very presence. This bread is available to all, Jew and Gentile alike, anyone who would come to His table.

The word "abide" used in John 6 is used elsewhere in John 15 where Jesus talks of the vine - the source of wine. The bread and the wine - the body and the blood. His presence is the true bread, His presence is the new wine.

It is the bread of His Presence that is food that will "never spoil," but "endures to eternal life." (John 6:27) This bread is eternal. Its life, blessing, and nourishment will only increase the more we partake.

Likewise, the new wine of His presence enables us to truly drink of His love, and in abiding in that love, enables and empowers us to bear the fruit for His Kingdom. (John 15:4, 10)

Jesus said that it was only eating the bread of His presence and drinking of the new wine of His love that will satisfy us. Once we have eaten and drunk of Him, we will never hunger or thirst again. (John 6:35) It is He that sustains us and fills us. He is the source of our joy and strength. He is the life giver. He is the One that nourishes us. He is our portion. He is our satisfaction.

> 'Jesus said to them, "Very truly I tell you, unless you eat the flesh of the Son of Man and drink his blood, you have no life in you. Whoever eats My flesh and drinks My blood has eternal life, and I will raise them up at the last day. For My flesh is real food and My blood is real drink. Whoever eats My flesh and drinks My blood remains in me, and I in them. Just as the living Father sent me and I live because of the Father, so the one who feeds on Me will live because of Me. This is the bread that came down from heaven. Your ancestors ate manna and died, but whoever feeds on this bread will live forever."' (v53-58)

> 'Only insofar as you eat and drink flesh and blood, the flesh and blood of the Son of Man, do you have life within you. The one who brings a hearty appetite to this eating and drinking has eternal life and will be fit and ready for the Final Day. My flesh is real food and My blood is real drink. By eating My flesh and drinking My blood you enter into me and I into you. In the same way that the fully alive Father sent Me here and I live because of Him, so the one who makes a meal of

Me lives because of Me. This is the Bread from heaven. Your ancestors ate bread and later died. Whoever eats this Bread will live always.' (The Mess)

When Jesus tells us to eat His flesh and drink His blood, we must be careful not to dismiss this as symbolism or metaphor. In fact He makes it very clear He was not using metaphor - my flesh is real food and my blood is real drink. "I am not being poetic here, I am speaking of something real, something tangible." He was not speaking of cannibalism of course, He was speaking of another reality, a spiritual reality, something that they could not understand with their natural understanding.

When we speak of eating of the body and blood of Christ at the Table are we speaking metaphorically? No! Are you saying the Bread and the Wine are literally the body and blood of Jesus? No, I am not saying that either! I am speaking of a spiritual reality that only the Holy Spirit can help us comprehend.
The Lord's Table is real food and real drink. Communion with Jesus is more than just a metaphor, it is real and it is powerful.

This is the most beautiful truth of all: not only do I dine with Him, but I dine of Him!

He is host of the Banquet, He is my dining companion; and He is also the food itself, He is the drink itself. He sits with me and offers me bread and wine, but He Himself is the bread and the wine. He offers me Himself.

A few years ago there was a television program called, "You Are What You Eat." The premise of the program was that the quality of food and drink you digest determines the health and the quality of someone's life.
As we eat and drink of Jesus at the Table, as I enjoy communion with Him I receive life. The word used for life in this passage, is Zoë. Zoë life is more than natural, physical life - it speaks of spiritual life, eternal life, the divine nature, the very life of

God Himself!

When the children of Israel ate and drank in the wilderness they did not realise it but 1 Corinthians tells us that ate "spiritual food" and drank "spiritual drink" (v3-4). The word "spiritual" is the Greek word pnemua, the same word for Holy Spirit. As they ate and drank they were receiving the very life and presence of the Holy Spirit! And this was just a shadow. The reality and full manifestation is for us! For those of us who would come to Jesus' Table.

As I eat the bread and drink the wine I receive the very life of God within me! My union with Him enables me to become a partaker of the divine nature! (2 Peter 1:4)

The life that we receive in communion is eternal life. For the believer, eternal life is not just a state that begins when we die, but something we begin to experience the moment we eat and drink of Christ. As we eat the bread and drink the wine we are tasting of the goodness of the Word of God and of the powers of the coming age. (Hebrews 6:5)

This is why there is a promise of physical healing that we can claim at the Lord's Table. In eternity there shall be no sickness, no pain, no disease and no death. At the Communion Table we are eating of that coming age, feeding on resurrection life, the divine life. We are enjoying the appetiser of the Great Wedding Banquet of the Lamb.

There is no death or disease in the Zoë life of the Spirit, and it is that life that we receive as we enjoy communion with Jesus.

For the believer, eternity starts at the Table. "This is eternal life," said Jesus "that they know you, the only true God, and Jesus Christ, whom you have sent." (John 17:3)

Eternal life is only found in communion, in relationship, in intimacy with God. Jesus said that unless we eat His flesh and drink His blood there is no life in us. You can never receive the life of God by by-passing communion. Only in the intimacy of communion is life found.

Acts 10:41 tells us that only those who ate and drank with Him were witnesses of His resurrection. It was those that enjoyed communion with Him that experienced His resurrection life, power, and glory. It seems that dining with Him is the precursor to resurrection life. This is not only an eschatological doctrine, but a present day experience – as I dine with Him and of Him, I experience resurrection life and power.

"I will raise them up at the last day." The Lord's Table is a prophetic act, reminding us of the future day of resurrection. Every time I partake of Communion I am reminding myself that this world is not my home. I am prophesying that Christ is coming, and that I will be resurrected with Him, and I will rule and reign with Him.

But remember, eternal life begins not at the Resurrection Day, but at the moment of communion. At the Table, I am feeding on the One who is the Resurrection and the Life. Therefore, every time I take Communion, I am being raised up. Every time I eat and drink of the presence of Jesus I am being raised up out of shame, out of fear, out of depression. I am being lifted to that place of being seated at the Table with Christ, in Heavenly Places. I am seeing things from Heaven's perspective.

"He who feeds on me will live," – on me. We don't just eat with Him – we eat of Him.

The phrase "feeds on" is the Greek word trogo and it is a verb. Jesus is speaking of a continual act of feeding on Him, looking to Him as our source and our portion, looking to communion with Him as the thing to sustain us and give us nourishment. It is this feasting on Christ that takes place at the Supper, by faith.

Jesus said that as we learn to do this we "abide in Him". Communion enables us to enter into Christ Himself, to abide in His Presence, dwell in His shadow, to truly know the reality of being in Christ and all the promises contained in that.

But not only does communion enable us to abide in Him, it also enables Him to abide in us. The very life of Christ Himself is imparted into us as we eat and drink of Him. If it is true that "you are what you eat," then the consequences for the ones who eat and drink of Christ are truly staggering!

Something of the power, glory and majesty of the risen Christ is imparted into me as I feed on Him. Even my mortal body is quickened as I receive resurrection life by communing with Him. His resurrection life has no cancer, no arthritis, no heart disease, and no sickness at all. It is this life that we are receiving. It is this life that we are feeding on. It is this life that is being imparted into us.

> *'Jesus, the real Jesus, the living Jesus who dwells in heaven and rules over the earth as well, the Jesus who has brought God's future into the present – wants not just to influence us, but to rescue us; not just to inform us, but to heal us; not just to give us something to think about, but to feed us, and to feed us with Himself. That's what this meal is all about.'*
> (How God Became King: The Forgotten Story of the Gospels – N. T. Wright)

A Prayer of Response

"Holy Spirit, as I eat this bread and drink this wine I receive into myself the very life and presence of Jesus. I receive His divine life and power, I receive the reality of His resurrection. I feast on the very presence of Jesus. Jesus, you offer me Yourself to eat, You offer me Yourself to drink. What more do I need? What more do I desire? In receiving you I receive Your grace and I receive Your strength. I receive Your healing power. I receive Your joy and peace. Raise me up. Sustain me. Empower me. I feast on all that You are, and now all that You are enters into me. Holy Spirit as I eat and drink of Jesus, heal my body, renew my soul, fill the very depths of my spirit with Your Presence. Amen."

"All the good that is in me is due to Holy Communion. I owe everything to it. I feel this holy fire has transformed me completely."

- *St. Faustina*

7

THE TABLE
THE PLACE OF TRANSPORTATION

"He has taken me to the banqueting table and his banner over me is love.'"

(Song of Songs 2:4)

In this chapter we are going to look at a story in the Old Testament from the life of David. We are going to begin in 2 Samuel 4. To give context to this verse, the king of Israel at this time is Saul and his son - the assumed future king - is Jonathan. However God's plan is for Saul to be removed from his throne and for David - the man after his own heart - to take his place. Both Saul and Jonathan are killed in battle at a place called Jezreel. It is in this context that we read the following verse:

'Jonathan son of Saul had a son who was lame in both feet. He was five years old when the news about Saul and Jonathan came from Jezreel. His nurse picked him up and fled, but as she hurried to leave, he fell and became disabled. His name was Mephibosheth.' (v4)

Talk about a bad nurse! You certainly wouldn't want her looking after your children! Now we are going to fast forward many years. David is now the King of Israel and secure in his position. The child Mephibosheth is now an adult and has a son of his own. Let's read the whole of 2 Samuel 9:

*David asked, 'Is there anyone still left of the house of Saul to
whom I can show kindness for Jonathan's sake?'*

*Now there was a servant of Saul's household named Ziba. They summoned
him to appear before David, and the king said to him, 'Are you Ziba?'
'At your service,' he replied.
The king asked, 'Is there no one still alive from the house of Saul
to whom I can show God's kindness?'
Ziba answered the king, 'There is still a son of Jonathan; he is lame in both feet.'
Where is he?' the king asked.
Ziba answered, 'He is at the house of Makir son of Ammiel in Lo Debar.'*

*So King David had him brought from Lo Debar, from the
house of Makir son of Ammiel.
When Mephibosheth son of Jonathan, the son of Saul, came to
David, he bowed down to pay him honour.*

*David said, 'Mephibosheth!'
'At your service,' he replied.*

*'Don't be afraid,' David said to him, 'for I will surely show you kindness for the
sake of your father Jonathan. I will restore to you all the land that belonged
to your grandfather Saul, and you will always eat at my table.'
Mephibosheth bowed down and said, 'What is your servant, that you
should notice a dead dog like me?'*

*Then the king summoned Ziba, Saul's steward, and said to him, 'I have given your
master's grandson everything that belonged to Saul and his family. You and your
sons and your servants are to farm the land for him and bring in the crops, so that*

your master's grandson may be provided for. And Mephibosheth, grandson of your master, will always eat at my table.' (Now Ziba had fifteen sons and twenty servants.)

Then Ziba said to the king, 'Your servant will do whatever my lord the king commands his servant to do.' So Mephibosheth ate at David's table like one of the king's sons.

Mephibosheth had a young son named Mika, and all the members of Ziba's household were servants of Mephibosheth. And Mephibosheth lived in Jerusalem, because he always ate at the king's table; he was lame in both feet.

Imagine for a moment that you were King David. You reign supreme over the monarchy of Israel. You can click your fingers and servants come running, granting your every wish and desire. You can decide to kill your enemies, build a new palace, or invade a neighbouring country. But as we look at the heart of David we see a king with a different spirit to the kings of this world. The only desire and request of this great king is, 'Is there anyone in my kingdom whom I can show kindness to?'

David's heart is a reflection of the heart of God, and David himself is a prophetic type of the King above all Kings, Jesus Christ. Jesus has all power and all authority. He can issue orders and angels do His bidding. He could click His fingers and destroy nations. He could withhold His breath and wipe out the planet. And yet when our King looks at us - pitiful creatures though we are at times - His heart bursts with the question, "Is there anyone in my Kingdom whom I can show kindness to?" This is His delight. This is His joy.

The word "kindness" used in this passage is the Hebrew word hesed. It is one of the most powerful and beautiful words used to describe the heart of God. Translated in some places as "love" and in other places as "kindness," in other places these two words are joined together and hesed is translated as "loving kindness." It is a rich word meaning grace, favour, and unconditional love.

This is the heart of our King! Rather than looking at His subjects with judgement or a desire to punish, His heart explodes with explodes with hesed towards you! He so longs to show someone His loving kindness, grace, favour, and unconditional love.

An Unexpected Recipient

Someone in David's kingdom would receive the kindness of the king that day, but perhaps it would be the most unlikely candidate of all: Mephibosheth. There were two major things that went against Mephibosheth - his lineage and his disability.

Firstly, remember who Mephibosheth's grandfather was - the previous king! It wouldn't have been uncommon for a new king on the throne - if he were from outside the previous royal family - to execute the members of the old king's family. That way he would establish his own throne, eliminate potential threats, and be able to build his own dynasty. In this context Mephibosheth might have expected to have been executed by David. He was the king's enemy, culturally deserving of death.

And yet instead this most unlikely of candidates became a recipient of the king's kindness! Instead of a sword Mephibosheth got shown love, mercy and kindness. Instead of a death sentence he got an invitation to a table!

In a similar way all of us have been born into this world as sinners. We are all objects of wrath, enemies of God, and deserving of death and hell. None of us could have any complaints if a holy and righteous God showed us judgement and punishment. And yet He decides to show mercy! He chooses to show grace! He delights to pour His loving kindness into us! Instead of sending us to hell, He longs to invite us to His

Table! This is our Jesus!

The second reason why Mephibosheth was the most unlikely candidate was because of his disability - he was lame in both feet. Disabled people weren't seen as being able to contribute to society, and so were often shunned, ignored and put out of the way, reduced to a life of begging and poverty. They were certainly not invited to palaces to dine with kings! Perhaps some even saw Mephibosheth's lameness as a punishment from God, and despised him because of what he had become.

And yet this broken, crippled man was ushered into the presence of the great king and invited to dine at his table. In this culture it was scandalous grace, reckless mercy.

As we look at the broken legs of Mephibosheth we are reminded of our own brokenness. Life has broken all of us in some way. The fall of Mephibosheth as a child is a reminder that we are all fallen creatures, living in a fallen world. Our sin and the sins of others has left us all broken, stumbling through life, walking with a limp. Maybe it was our stupid choices or mistakes that left us broken. Maybe - like with Mephibosheth - we are broken through no fault of our own. Maybe the words and actions of a friend, a spouse, a partner, a boss, or just the circumstances of life have left us wounded and broken. Maybe, like Mephibosheth, the person who was meant to be looking after you: a teacher, parent, or pastor ended up hurting you and leaving you broken.

Thank God that our King doesn't ignore the broken ones amongst us! Instead the broken, hurting, wounded, crippled, and limping ones are the very ones He loves to invite to His Table. It is the lost, the abused, the divorced, the addicts, the ones living in shame, the ones who life has left shattered - the King is calling them to His Table!

Everything Changes

I wonder what Mephibosheth's first reaction was when he woke to find that he had an invitation from the king. Perhaps fear, or shame. Whatever he initially thought, he decided to respond to that invitation and travel to Jerusalem and enter the presence of the king. When he arrived, he bowed down before David showing honour, submission, and respect.

What happened next would change everything! Something amazing happens when we respond to the King's invitation to come into His presence. When we come in humility and surrender, bowing down at His feet in worship we find something staggering. We have not come to a throne of judgement, but a Table of mercy. We have not come as servants, but as dining companions. We have not become part of a once a week religious church service, but we have entered into a lifestyle of intimate communion with God.

The first thing that would change for Mephibosheth was that he literally moved house! The location of the king's table was significant. Mephibosheth would have his location changed in an instant. The Bible tells us that Mephibosheth lived in a place called Lo Debar. The name Lo Debar means "a pasture-less place". Lo Debar was a place that was dry, barren, lonely and isolated. It was the kind of place where you planted much but reaped little. Not the kind of place you wanted to live, especially for a farmer like Mephibosheth. It was a hard and difficult environment.

Imagine the shock then, when David tells Mephibosheth, "As we speak, the removal men are outside your house! In order to dine at my table, you will have to come to live with me in Jerusalem!" Jerusalem means the "city of peace." The Hebrew word for peace, shalom, means more than just peace; it means "wholeness, completeness, nothing broken, nothing undone."
Mephibosheth wasn't just going to Jerusalem for a holiday, he was going to live

there forever. Overnight he was literally transported to the place of his dreams!

Many of us can relate to Mephibosheth. We too know what it is to live in Lo Debar. For many of us it seems we live a life that seems dry and barren. Many of us know what it is to struggle and get by, planting much but reaping little. For many of us life is just tough. It's hard. It's difficult. For many of us "the winter season" has become a lifestyle of winter; the wilderness the place we have camped in for far too long.
But at the Table something remarkable happens - we find that our location changes! We find that we have come to "the heavenly Jerusalem....to thousands upon thousands of angels in joyful assembly, to the Church of the firstborn, whose names are written in Heaven. You have come to God, the Judge of all, to the spirits of the righteous made perfect, to Jesus the mediator of a new covenant." (Hebrews 12:22-24) We find that "the Jerusalem that is above is free, and she is our mother". We find that "we have a building from God, an eternal house…not built by human hands." (2 Corinthians 5:1) We have been transported from Lo Debar and are now "seated with Him in the heavenly realms in Christ Jesus." The King proclaims that we are leaving Lo Debar and we are never going back there! He declares over us "the winter is past; the rains are over and gone." (Song of Songs 2:11)

As we respond to the King's invitation and sit at His table we find that we leave Lo Debar for good. You cannot eat at the King's Table and remain in Lo Debar. To go to one is to leave the other. As long as I am at the King's Table, I never even have to visit Lo Debar again. Jerusalem is now my home. I am in a place of peace, a place of wholeness, I am complete at the Table.

Transportation

We will return to the story of Mephibosheth shortly, but for now I want to continue to look at the idea that the Table is a place of transportation. People like Elijah and Philip were literally transported by God from one physical location and relocated to another. God can do things like that! He's awesome that way! Although the idea of being physically transported in an instant from one location to another may be appealing, (a beach Lord, with palm trees and lots of sun!) but if we are honest we know that just changing physical locations doesn't change the inner person, the real us. What we need is a spiritual location shift. We need to be transported out of our shame, guilt, fear, unworthiness, and barrenness and be transported into a place of wholeness, joy, freedom, and security. The good news is that the same God who is able to physically transport people from one location to the next, is well able to lift us out of our Lo Debar and transport us into a whole new realm of emotional and spiritual wellbeing. He does this at the Table.

In the same way that David's table, transported Mephibosheth to living conditions that were beyond his wildest dreams, our King's Table transports us to a place of such joy, freedom, and hope!

This imagery is used so powerfully in Song of Songs 2. The whole book of Song of Songs is about the communion and intimacy of a Bride and Bridegroom. The prophetic language of the Communion Table and the transportation that takes place when we go there is made so clear in verse 4: "Let him lead me to the banquet hall, and let his banner over me be love." The New King James phrases it: "He brought me to the banqueting house." Both of these speak of the gentle leading and wooing of the King who ushers us into that place of communion with Himself.

The fact that I am brought implies permission, an invitation and access. The fact that "He" brought me implies that He enabled me to come; it is a work of grace, a work of the Spirit.

The Passion Translation perhaps uses more dramatic language: "Suddenly, he transported me into his house of wine - he looked upon me with his unrelenting love divine."

"Suddenly, he transported me" - it is the language of rapture, of being snatched away, of being removed from one place and taken to another. It is a sudden, immediate moment of transformation. In an instant everything has changed!

So where was the Bride in Song of Songs being transported from? The preceding verses describe her as being like "a lily among thorns," (v2). This was her location - among the thorns. She is surrounded by all the effects of the curse: death, pain, sickness, sin, separation. She was in a harsh, barren, painful environment. She was trapped and couldn't get out.

Then in a moment everything changed! She left the thorns behind, left the desert behind! Suddenly she was transported to the King's table! Taken to a place of comfort, delight, beauty, and blessing.

At the table she found that there was beautiful fruit for her to eat: "His fruit is sweet to my taste," and "Sweet and delicious to my palate." - Amp (v3).

There were raisins and apples for her to eat and it is this fruit that "strengthened" her (v5). The Hebrew word for strengthen here is the word samak. It means "To lay one's hand upon, to lean upon, to be made steadfast or to gain confidence."

What a beautiful picture this is. As I lean into Him at the Table, He lays His hand upon me! It is a moment of powerful impartation as divine strength is infused into me, and I am made steadfast. This is now my confidence and security - I am seated with My King at the Table.

Interestingly the word used for "raisins" is the Hebrew word ba'ashishot, which can also be translated "fires". Surely as we dine with Him and dine of Him, the fires of His love and passion burn within us; the flames of His Spirit, immerse and engulf us. What a baptism takes place at the Table! A baptism of fire, love, and passion!

Not only was she strengthened at the table, but she was refreshed also. Not only was there food to eat to strengthen her but there was wine to drink to refresh her. What a contrast between living amongst thorns (giving the impression of a dry and barren environment) to being in a place where she was refreshed and revived.

The phrase "banqueting hall" can also be translated "the house of wine." It was in this secret location that the finest of wines were stored. The bridegroom made sure that his bride had access to the house of wine, and could drink freely of the finest wines that were available in the kingdom. In the same way the Bride of Christ has been given access to the wine, not to the wine of this world that leads to debauchery, but the wine of heaven, which we can drink freely. (Ephesians 5:18) We can drink of the Spirit until we are so full that He becomes out of us a mighty river that flows. (John 7:37-39)

Throughout Song of Songs the bride compares the drinking of wine with experiencing the love of her bridegroom. More than the food on the table, what she really wants is to experience his love. "I am faint with love" (v5) - she finds his love so overwhelming and intense that she literally cannot stand upright in the presence of this love. The King James Version describes her as being "lovesick," while the Passion Translation records her confession as, 'I am longing for more–yet how could I take more?'

This is much more than a fleeting romance, more than just butterflies in the stomach - this is a love of such depth, intensity, and passion that it is almost too much for her to handle. We need to experience Jesus in such a way! To the unconverted this type of language might seem foolish. To the religious it might sound like heresy or irreverence. But God so longs for us to discover Him in this way. He longs to knock us off of our feet and overwhelm us by His intense, all consuming love. As Rick Pino described it in his song, Your Love Is Like:

> Your love is like the rain falling on my soul
> Covering every place, making gardens grow
> Sweetness overflows, pouring from Your lips
> Kisses from above, let the heavens drip
>
> Your love is like the ocean
> I'm drowning in Your presence
> I'm getting lost in the gaze of Your eyes
> I'm getting lost in the warmth of Your smile
>
> Your love is like a room full of precious jewels
> It takes my breath away, there's riches beyond words
> When it's just me and You, I can't remember storms
> All I can do is melt into Your arms

It is this love that becomes her banner (v4). In that culture; kings, tribes, armies, and so forth, were all identified by their distinctive banners. In saying that his love has become her banner, not only is she saying that his love is her protection and her covering, but she is saying that his love has become her identity.

It is important for us to understand that our primary identity is that we are loved by Jesus. I am the "disciple that Jesus loves," (John 13:23) reclining next to Him at the Table. As Brennan Manning puts it in The Ragamuffin Gospel: "My deepest awareness of myself is that I am deeply loved by Jesus Christ." And in Abba's Child: "Define yourself radically as one beloved by God. This is the true self. Every other identity is illusion."

At the Table every other banner that is over my life fades away. I am no longer Andrew Murray, the evangelist, the preacher, the author, the struggling saint, the recovering sinner - I am loved by Jesus. This is who I am. This is my identity. This is the only banner that matters. This is all that counts. I may be surrounded by guilt and shame and daily reminded of my failures, but at the Table I look up and see a banner over my head and I whisper, "I am the disciple that Jesus loves."

My Lover and My Friend

'Let him kiss me with the kisses of his mouth -
for your love is more delightful than wine.' (Song of Songs 1:2)

Once again, the love of the Bridegroom is compared to wine. To experience His love is something that is joyful and sweet, but there is also an addictive quality to it. To experience His love is not a one-time thing, but contained within the love of God is a quality that causes us to continually yearn for more. We have to keep coming back, keep experiencing, keep going deeper. I am both full and satisfied, and ravenously hungry and thirsty for more!

The Hebrew word for "love" in this verse is the word dod. This is the most common word for love used in the Song of Songs. This word for love is the word used for a love between friends. It is interesting that within language that is at times intimate and sexual that there is also a link with this particular form of love. The relationship in Song of Songs is both one of physical attraction, and also one of deep friendship. On one hand, the love of the Bridegroom is exciting and exhilarating, but it is also strong, comforting, stable, and secure; "this is my lover, this is my friend." (5:6)

The Bridegroom describes this love as more "delightful than wine." (1:2) The English word "delightful" is the Hebrew word yatab. It means that which is pleasing, good, excellent, lovely, joyful, fruitful, precious, cheerful, kind, and righteous! What a perfect description of the immeasurable love of Jesus!

A different word for "delight" is used in Chapter 2, Verse 3, "I delight to sit in his shade." Here the word hamad is used which means to "long for." Her pursuit in life, the thing that she longed for more than anything else was to sit at his table, dining with him. That for her had become her shade - her safety, the place where she could be at rest whilst being overwhelmed and overshadowed by His presence. This for her had become her "great delight."

It was at the table that she found her greatest moments of intimacy. It was here she found "his left arm is under my head, and his right arm embraces me." (v6) At the Table He embraces me, He holds me close to His heart, He literally pulls me into Himself. No place is more intimate. No place is more glorious.

In his commentary on Song of Songs, Watchman Nee writes:

'I sat down under his shadow with great delight.' Great delight may be translated 'rapture.' Sitting under His shadow signifies a tremendous lifting up of spirit - an ecstatic delight in His presence which gives the feeling of being taken up in rapture.

The Bride found herself invited to the banqueting table of the king. As she responded to his invitation, she suddenly found herself raptured, transported away from living amongst thorns to a place of ecstatic joy, and intense, overwhelming love.

In the same way, as Mephibosheth was invited to the king's table, he found himself transported from the place of struggle and barrenness to the place of peace and wholeness.

When we take our place at the Lord's Table we may not physically change locations, but in the Spirit we have been transported to another dimension. We are in the presence of Almighty God - the place of ultimate love, joy, and freedom. We have found our home in His presence, sitting under His shadow and living in our new identity as His beloved.

Truly in that place we hear this song sung over us:

*The season has changed,
the bondage of your barren winter has ended,
and the season of hiding is over and gone.
The rains have soaked the earth
and left it bright with blossoming flowers.
The season for singing and pruning the vines has arrived.
I hear the cooing of doves in our land,
filling the air with songs to awaken you
and guide you forth.*

*Can you not discern this new day of destiny
breaking forth around you?
The early signs of my purposes and plans
are bursting forth.
The budding vines of new life*

are now blooming everywhere.
The fragrance of their flowers whispers,
"There is change in the air."

Arise, my love, my beautiful companion,
and run with me to the higher place.
For now is the time to arise and come away with me.
(Song of Songs 2:11-13) TPT

A Prayer of Response

"Jesus I hear you inviting me, gently wooing me to Your Table. I respond to Your call and come worshipfully and humbly into Your Presence. Oh Jesus, as I come to Your Table I leave behind my barrenness, I leave behind the struggle, the heartache and the pain. I leave the cold of my winter season. I leave my sin and my shame behind. I come into Your glorious presence where there is light and life. Here I am made whole. Here I am made complete. Oh Jesus, let me truly drink deeply of Your love. Overwhelm me with Your love. Hold me close. Kiss me. Embrace me. Satisfy my every longing and desire. You are my friend and my lover. I am the one that you love. Your love is my greatest joy. You are my everything. Amen."

"From now on, near the Eucharist I shall be able to…wait for heaven in peace, keeping myself open to the rays of the Divine Host. In this furnace of love I shall be consumed."

- *St. Theresa of Lisieux*

8

THE TABLE
A PLACE OF TRANSFORMATION

"And Mephibosheth lived in Jerusalem, because he always ate at the king's table; he was lame in both feet."

(2 Samuel 9:13)

We are now going to return to the beautiful and powerful story of Mephibosheth in 2 Samuel. As we saw in the previous chapter, Mephibosheth was the unlikely beneficiary of the kindness of the king. A man that was a cripple would have been ignored by most of society, but he was invited to dine at the king's table. He was of the lineage of Saul and so would have been considered an enemy of David, but was surprisingly invited to a place of fellowship and communion.

As Mephibosheth responded to the invitation of the king we saw in the previous chapter that this would mean a location change for him. He left Lo Debar, the place of struggle and hardship and was transported to Jerusalem, the city of peace and wholeness.

Change of Position

Not only did David's invitation mean a location change but it meant a positional change too. In Lo Debar, Mephibosheth lived in the house of a man called Makir, son of Ammiel. This man is not mentioned in Scripture again so he appears an insignificant character. Mephibosheth was perhaps a lodger in this man's house. It was quite a demotion for a son of a prince to find himself living in these humble, unassuming surroundings.

But everything changed when he moved to Jerusalem. Now not only had his location changed, but his position had changed - he was now dining with royalty! He was eating at the king's table!

Imagine the pomp and ceremony that takes place at a royal banquet, imagine the security arrangements. Not everyone is allowed the privilege of dining with a king. There are protocols in place. Only the best are honoured with this kind of invitation.

Imagine the shock among the royal family, the guards, and the officials in court as the doors opened, and in came a man, crippled in both feet. He didn't even have the ability to walk to the table himself without assistance. You could hear the mumbling and complaining, and then as they studied his face they realised that this was the grandson of none other than David's arch enemy - King Saul. How did he dare enter the king's presence? Who did he think he was? Things got even more shocking. As Mephibosheth was carried in, they lifted him closer and closer to the king himself. Then they looked at the empty chair at the king's table. Surely not, they thought. But yes, Mephibosheth was seated at the head table, the place of honour, of prestige and privilege. Every head nervously turned towards the king. Was this approved by him? He smiled. This man was not hijacking the kings meal, he was the king's special guest. He had been invited and he had been welcomed.

Only one word can sum up this situation - grace! The remarkable and astounding grace, the hesed, the loving kindness of the king - that the most undeserving of all had found a seat at his table.

As an evangelist who travels around the world, I will often find myself travelling by plane. I have discovered that planes have a similar structure and layout. At the front is the first class cabin, where the expensive seats are. It is a better travel experience, with more spacious seats, better service, and better quality food.

Alas, I have never travelled first class! My seat is normally at the back! It is here, in the cheapest seats that the experience is the most basic and can sometimes be uncomfortable and unpleasant. But there is something that can occasionally happen when you travel - an invitation called a free upgrade! A free upgrade is when you have paid for a cheaper seat, but then you are suddenly ushered into the first class cabin. The generosity of the airline means that you have been given a seat that you did not pay for and that you don't deserve.

The invitation to the King's Table is the greatest free upgrade of all! Christ is Himself seated at the right hand of the Father in Heaven. (Colossians 3:1) He is seated in a place of victory, of authority, a place where He rules and reigns.

And here is the stunning invitation of the gospel - you get to sit at His table! Paul puts it like this in Ephesians 2:6, "God raised us up with Christ and seated us with Him in the heavenly realms in Christ Jesus."

What an invitation! I am now seated in a seat of blessing, of abundance, and of favour. I am in a seat of forgiveness and righteousness. I am in a seat free of shame and condemnation. I have been brought from my seat of darkness and am now seated in the light. I am seated in healing, in joy, and in peace. I am in a seat of victory and authority where I am more than a conqueror. I am the head and not the tail and no weapon formed against me shall prosper!

Not only that, but I get to dine with the King of Kings and the Lord of Lords! Surely the words of David ring true for us all, 'He raises the poor from the dust and lifts the needy from the ash heap; He seats them with princes and has them inherit a throne of honour.' (1 Samuel 2:8)

This is the best upgrade - available for all! All are invited and welcome at His table.

An Identity Transformation

'So Mephibosheth ate at David's table like one of the king's sons.' (2 Samuel 9:11)

This is one of the most powerful aspects of this story. Mephibosheth got to eat at the king's table, but not as an inferior guest. He was not treated as a curiosity at a freak show. David's acceptance of Mephibosheth extended to him being adopted and treated as one of the king's sons.

Not only had Mephibosheth's location changed and his place changed – but now his identity changed too. This is the greatest transformation of all. Our circumstances can change but if we are still tied to our old identity then we will never truly be free. In being adopted into the royal family, Mephibosheth's transformation was truly complete.

The name Mephibosheth means "a shameful thing." Can you imagine being called that by your parents? All his life, Mephibosheth had lived feeling like a shameful thing. The shame of his disability, the shame of his past, the shame of who his grandfather was. All his life he had lived with a sense of guilt, feeling no good, worthless, a loser. No wonder he described himself to David as a "dead dog." This is how he saw himself. He looked at himself and saw no sense of value whatsoever.

But at the king's table everything changed. Although he called himself David's servant, David would call him his son! He was no longer the dead dog, or the shameful thing - he was the son of a king! He was given royal robes to wear! The sons of kings are treated with honour. They have a dignity about them. They have authority. They have favour. They have respect. They are blessed. Their identity is one of value.

In a moment this man's entire identity - how he saw himself and how others saw him - was changed. He was given a brand new identity. One far greater than anything he could ask, think or imagine.

Many of us have lived with an identity of shame, of fear, of uselessness; of being ashamed or embarrassed of who we are or what we have done. Many of us can't see any value in who we are. But the King of Kings longs to strip away from us any identity that isn't found in Him. For in Him we are sons and daughters of God! We are royalty. We have been chosen and adopted into His family, into His Kingdom. We can call the King, Abba - daddy. We have been given worth and value. We have been honoured, favoured and blessed. We have been lifted to an exalted place where we have dignity and acceptance. This is the miracle that takes place at the King's Table - those who see themselves as dead dogs, suddenly find themselves in royal robes, as sons and daughters of God, royalty in the Kingdom of Heaven.

As we dine with the King, we don't need to sit feeling like we don't belong or we are not good enough. He has called us His own. He has made us worthy. He accepts us and welcomes us as His very children. Indeed our Saviour is 'not ashamed to call them (us) brothers.'

The Decree of the King

The transformation in the life of Mephibosheth reminds me of another amazing turn around in the Scriptures. The last king of Judah was a man called Jehoiachin. In around 3000 BC the Babylonian armies of Nebuchadnezzar invaded Jerusalem. The city was destroyed and thousands of Jews were taken as captives back to Babylon.

Jehoiachin lost everything that day. Lost his crown and his throne. Lost his royal position and privilege. He was taken miles from his homeland where he was made a spectacle before a foreign people. In shame he was thrown into a prison where he was kept under lock and key for 37 years!

Can you imagine being in a dungeon for 37 years? We can only imagine the mental state of Jehoiachin, but I am sure that with every year that passed his hopes of release grew fainter and fainter. By his fourth decade of captivity, all hopes would have faded. As far as he was concerned he was going to die in this prison.

And then one day everything changed! Jeremiah 52 records the incredible transformation that took place in this man's circumstances:

> 'In the thirty-seventh year of the exile of Jehoiachin king of Judah, in the year Awel-Marduk became king of Babylon, on the twenty-fifth day of the twelfth month, he released Jehoiachin king of Judah and freed him from prison. He spoke kindly to him and gave him a seat of honour higher than those of the other kings who were with him in Babylon. So Jehoiachin put aside his prison clothes and for the rest of his life ate regularly at the king's table. Day by day the king of Babylon gave Jehoiachin a regular allowance as long as he lived, till the day of his death.' (v31-34)

In one moment the king proclaimed a decree over Jehoiachin's life and everything changed! For the first time in 37 years he had no chains. He left prison behind and saw the light of the sun again. He was free. Instead of the harsh words of the jailors, the king spoke words of grace and kindness to him - words of hesed. He was given a seat of honour and privilege. Value, worth, and a sense of his royal birth-right were restored back to him. Even financial provision was his. But most significantly of all, he was given the right to dine with the king, and commune at the table.

Perhaps some reading this have felt like they were living in a prison. A prison of shame, or fear, or low self-esteem. Maybe you have lived in a prison of addiction, or of depression or anxiety. Whatever it is, it's like you are trapped and can't get out. Maybe you have lived in this prison for nearly 40 years, maybe your whole life. Perhaps it's reached the point where you no longer believe that freedom is possible.

I want to encourage you today that in a moment everything can change! The King of all Kings is calling you to His Table. He is calling you to leave your prison and be seated with Him. The seat at His Table is one of freedom, one of honour, one of provision, one of dignity. He is calling you to leave behind the prison clothes, and put on His royal robes. The exchange of garments is an exchange of identity. Old things have gone and all things have become new. You are no longer bound, you are no longer a slave - you are a child of the King! Seated at His Table, He longs to whisper in your ear words of kindness, affirming you as His son and daughter.

The King makes a new decree over you today - "You are My son, you are My daughter. You are loved, accepted, chosen, and forgiven. Leave behind the prison cell, leave behind your chains, leave behind your prison clothes. Sit here with Me. Dine with Me, fellowship with Me at My Table. Your captivity is over. You are free!"

Free From Restrictions

Jehoiachin was not the only one of God's people to be put in prison. Throughout the Bible, both in the Old and New Testament there are stories of God's servants that found themselves in a prison. A prison speaks of a place of restriction or limitation. There is a powerful verse in the book of Job that speaks of how God want to break us free from restrictions in our lives.

> *'He is wooing you from the jaws of distress to a spacious place free from restriction.' (Job 36:16)*

Restrictions and limitations. Have you ever found yourself longing to do something for God but that desire has been followed by a but, or an if? "If I had the money," "If I had the time," "If I had the energy," "But I'm too old," "But I'm too young," "But my mistakes have disqualified me," "But I'm not good enough," "But I tried it before and it didn't work." The desire speaks of God's destiny that He placed in us, but the but's and the if's speak of limitations and restrictions that the devil or other people have placed upon us. Or perhaps we have put those restrictions on ourselves.

The enemy loves to trap us in a prison of limitation or restriction. Sin, addiction, fear, guilt, shame, sickness, poverty, anxiety, depression, or a poor self-image - all these things can become crippling areas of restriction and limitation in our lives that paralyse us and stop us moving forward into everything that God has for us.

This verse speaks specifically of the "jaws of distress." The Hebrew word used here for "distress" speaks of confinement and restriction, and the jaws are of course what we use to speak. God is dealing here with words that limit and restrict us. Words like "you are useless," "you are a failure," "you'll never achieve anything," or "it'll never work." Some of us have lived our whole lives confined, restricted and limited by the words that have been spoken over us or the words we have spoken over ourselves.

But this verse provides us with an incredible promise - that God is wooing us to a place where we are free from restrictions. Can you imagine being brought to a place where every limitation and every restriction was broken? Can you imagine if everything that had been stopping you, everything that was holding you back was suddenly removed?

All the fears, all the shame, all the lack, all the anxiety, all the excuses - gone, lifted. Imagine the power of those negative words just being broken. There is a place that God is wooing us to where we are truly free - a spacious place, where we experience His delight. (2 Samuel 22:22)

But where is this place? Where is this place where restrictions and limitations no longer have a hold over me? Job 36 tells us exactly where this place is:

> *'He is wooing you from the jaws of distress to a spacious place free from restriction,* **to the comfort of your table laden with choice food.***'* *(v16)*

The spacious place, free from restrictions, is none other than the Table of the Lord. It is at the Communion Table that restrictions and limitations are lifted off of us. When I am dining with the Lord, there is an anointing that is present at His table that destroys every yoke. He is there to set the captives free and to break every chain. Where the Spirit of the Lord is there is freedom. So if I am where He is, if I am communing and fellowshipping with Him at His table, how can I remain bound? How can I remain restricted and limited in my walk with Him?

Despite the words of the enemy that limit and restrict, at the Table our King speaks His words of kindness over us and His words break the power of every other word. His proclamation is 'He who the Son sets free is free indeed.'

Our Response

God is a God who so longs to lead us to that place where we are free from all restrictions and limitations. His love is limitless, His grace is limitless, His power is limitless. There are no limits to what God can do in us and through us. He is a God who is able to do 'immeasurably more than all we ask or imagine, according to His power that is at work within us.' (Ephesians 3:20) He blesses us with EVERY spiritual blessing, gives us life and life in abundance, tells us that with Him ALL things are possible and give us His Spirit without limit or measure.

'For out of His fullness [the superabundance of His grace and truth] we have all received grace upon grace [spiritual blessing upon spiritual blessing, favour upon favour, and gift heaped upon gift].' (John 1:16 - Amp)

All of this is received at the Table, which is the place where God wants us. It is only in communion with the Lord, in encountering His presence that we experience true freedom. The word curse literally means "to limit or restrict." At the Cross, Jesus became the curse for us. He took upon Himself every limitation and restriction that the enemy tries to put on us so that we can know true freedom and His limitless amazing promises. It is at the Table, as we partake of the Lord's body and blood that all He achieved on the cross is applied to our lives.

God is wooing us to the Table. That means He is inviting us, drawing us, urging us - but the choice is yours. I remember a lady once telling me that she was once sat on a flight where she was offered a free upgrade to first class. However she turned it down! Sitting with her friend, there was only one upgraded seat available and she chose the company of her friend instead of the luxury of the upgrade. Whilst in the natural this may have been kind and noble, turning down God's free upgrade is foolishness. And yet there are many who ignore the promptings to come to the Table and have communion with their Lord. They have plenty of excuses as to why they cannot come, but meanwhile their place at the King's Table remains empty. They remain in their seat of bondage, lack and limitation. But the Holy Spirit never stops wooing us, never stops urging us, never stops drawing us to that place of true fellowship and intimacy with Jesus. Will you go there now? Will you respond to that wooing of the Holy Spirit? Seated at His Table - everything changes.

His Covenant

Returning to the story of Mephibosheth in 2 Samuel 9, we find ourselves asking an important question, why? Why would David do all that he did for Mephibosheth? Why would Jesus do what He has done for any of us? Mephibosheth not only got to dine at the king's table but he became one of the king's sons. Not only that but David promised to restore unto him all the land that had once belonged to Saul. Thank God that our King is still in the restoration business! He longs to restore joy and health and peace to people. He loves to restore families. He loves to restore faith and hope and purpose. He loves to restore people's identities.

Perhaps as Mephibosheth lay in bed that first night in Jerusalem and on other nights that followed there was an overwhelming sense of why? "What on earth have I done to deserve all of this?" Sometimes one of the things that will stop people from receiving all that God has for them is a sense that somehow they don't deserve it.

But as you look closely at the motivations of David in this passage you realise that it was never about Mephibosheth - it was always about Jonathan. "For Jonathan's sake" is a phrase repeated throughout the passage. You see many years earlier, David had entered into a covenant with Mephibosheth's father, Jonathan. It was a covenant that pledged that they would always show kindness to each other's descendants. Now even though many years had passed and David was well established as king over Israel, he never forgot the covenant he had made with Jonathan. This story was never about how deserving Mephibosheth was - it was all about the fact that David was a covenant keeping king.
When Jesus shed His blood at the Cross He entered into covenant with you. You may

not be deserving of the kindness of the King, but it's not about you, it's about Him! It's about the fact that He always remembers and keeps His covenant. Even when we don't deserve it, He still invites us to His table, He still dines with us, He still calls us His own.

When Mephibosheth came into court that day everyone in the room saw a cripple, but when David looked, perhaps He saw something different. Perhaps he looked into Mephibosheth's eyes and saw his father, Jonathan. And David looked, and remembered.

When we come to our King's table, perhaps we see our faults and our mistakes and our unworthiness, but the King sees something different. He sees His own image reflected in us. He looks at His hands and feet, and sees the wounds and the scars, and He remembers. He remembers the covenant He made. And He says "That's why I'm doing this."

You see the beautiful ending to this story is that as Mephibosheth takes his place, seated at the king's table, the table covers his broken feet. The thing that for him was a source of pain, a sign of his limitation, and a reminder of his past, was covered as he sat at the table. No one could see his brokenness, no one could see the thing that brought him so much shame. He sat covered, an equal with royalty.

Peter tells us that 'love covers over a multitude of sins.' (1 Peter 4:8) Whilst Proverbs tell us that "love covers over all wrongs." (Proverbs 10:12) Sins that we have committed, wrongs that have been done to us: Our King never exposes our weaknesses but He covers us, loves us, heals us and makes us whole. You can't see my weakness at the Table - at the Table I am a son of the King. I am loved. I am accepted. I am whole.
The band Leeland tell the story of Mephibosheth so beautifully in their song "Carried

To The Table." I will close this chapter by sharing the lyrics with you:

Wounded and forsaken
I was shattered by the fall
Broken and forgotten
Feeling lost and all alone
Summoned by the King
Into the Master's courts
Lifted by the Saviour
And cradled in His arms

I was carried to the table
Seated where I don't belong
Carried to the table
Swept away by His love
And I don't see my brokenness anymore
When I'm seated at the table of the Lord
I'm carried to the table
The table of the Lord

Fighting thoughts of fear
And wondering why He called my name
Am I good enough to share this cup
This world has left me lame
Even in my weakness
The Saviour called my name
In His Holy presence
I'm healed and unashamed
I was carried to the table

> Seated where I don't belong
> Carried to the table
> Swept away by His love
> And I don't see my brokenness anymore
> When I'm seated at the table of the Lord
> I'm carried to the table
> The table of the Lord
>
> You carried me, my God
> You carried me

Sometimes we come running to the Table, other times we are so broken that we come limping. Other times we don't have the strength to even do that. That is when we find His everlasting arms underneath us, carrying us to the Table, God bringing us to Himself. In that place He covers me. In that place He transforms me. I am no longer the same. I am changed by His love, in His presence, at His Table. Truly, what a wonderful Saviour is Jesus!

A Prayer of Response

"Precious Father, I don't have the strength to come to Your Table. I am broken, crippled by sin, wounded by this world. Father, hold me in Your arms and carry me to Your Table. Cover me with Your grace. Restore to me all that has been lost and stolen. Oh God, thank You that I can call you Father. I am a child of the King. In royal robes I don't deserve. I receive all that You have for me Father. Here in Your presence I am no longer bound by limitations and restrictions. You have brought me to a spacious place and I rejoice in Your freedom. Thank You Jesus for making a way. Thank You Father that You are truly a covenant keeping God. Amen."

"To converse with You, O King of glory, no third person is needed. You are always ready in the Sacrament of the Altar to give audience to all. All who desire You always find You there, and converse with You face to face."

- St. Theresa of Avila

9

THE TABLE
WHERE I FIGHT MY BATTLES

"Then the king asked, "What is it, Queen Esther? What is your request? Even up to half the kingdom, it will be given you.""

(Esther 5:3)

The book of Esther is not a book you would normally associate with the Lord's Supper. But hidden within this story is one of the great secrets of the power of Communion. Once we discover this I believe we will never approach the Communion table in the same way again.

The story of Esther is set in the kingdom of Persia where the Jewish people were in Exile. The king of the Persian Empire at this time was the mighty Xerxes. The culture of foreign kings at that time would have allowed for Xerxes to have a harem of many beautiful women, and from the harem, he would choose one to be the royal bride. A position of close proximity to the king and a role bringing great favour and honour. The royal bride at the start of the book is Queen Vashti.

Due to her disobedience, Vashti was deposed as Queen and a search for a new royal bride was undertaken. The young girl Esther or Hadassah (secretly a Jew) is chosen, and she becomes the new favourite of the king.

In the kingdom at that time was a wicked man called Haman. A descendant of the Amalekites (historical enemies of the Jews), Haman was an evil man who would stop at nothing until he had wiped out every single Jew from the kingdom. Through trickery and manipulation, Haman found the ear of the king and helped bring into law that on a certain day every Jew from the oldest to the youngest would be annihilated.

This was a terrifying moment for the Jewish people, powerless to defend themselves in a foreign land and facing complete extinction. There only hope was for someone to go into the presence of the king and beg for mercy.

A wise Jew by the name of Mordecai - the cousin of Queen Esther - approached her and told her of the situation. He begs her to go into the presence of the king and plead for the lives of her people. Esther knows that to approach the king without being summoned could result in death, so she is initially reluctant, however Mordecai persuades her with the famous words, "Who knows that you have come to royal position for such a time as this?" (Esther 4:14)

The Question

Esther called the Jews to pray and fast for her for three days so that she would find favour with the king. After the time of prayer and fasting was over, the Bible records the following:

'On the third day Esther put on her royal robes and stood in the inner court of the palace, in front of the king's hall. The king was sitting on his royal throne in the hall, facing the entrance. When he saw Queen Esther standing in the court, he was pleased with her and held out to her the gold sceptre that was in his hand. So Esther approached and touched the tip of the sceptre.' (5:1-2)

Imagine the relief that flooded Esther's soul, as she realised that she had found favour with the king! Then things got even better as the king asked her this incredible question:

'Then the king asked, "What is it, Queen Esther? What is your request? Even up to half the kingdom, it will be given you."' (v3)

Just pause for a moment and ponder that question. Esther has been given permission to ask for literally anything. The richest, most powerful, most influential person on the planet has just told her that she can ask for anything and he will give it to her. This is not just words, this man has the ability to fulfil any desire that she has!

What would you ask for? Imagine that you are in the company of the richest businessman or the most powerful president or the most influential celebrity and they look at you and say, "Ask me for ANYTHING and I will give it you." Cash - it's yours. A new house - it's yours. Your own tropical island paradise - it's yours. Whatever you want, name it, and it's yours.

Of course such a scenario is pure fantasy. But in one sense it isn't. As believers we have been given access, not into the presence of an earthly king or president, but into the presence of the King of Kings and the Lord of Lords. We have been called into the presence of the Creator of the heavens and the earth, the One with all power and all authority. He is the Name above all names and the One for whom nothing is impossible.

As the Church, we come into His presence as His royal bride. We have found favour in His sight, He has extended the royal sceptre. We can come boldly before His throne (Hebrews 4:16) and He has asked us to ask of Him. The New Testament is full of wonderful promises such as "ask and it will be given to you" (Matthew 7:7);

"ask whatever you wish, and it will be given you" (John 15:7); "my Father will give whatever you ask in My name." (John 16:23)

So what are you going to ask for today? If you are in the presence of the One who is able to give anything - which you are - and He is giving you permission to ask for anything - which He is - what are you going to ask for?

I guess for many of us our minds are filled with all kinds of requests and desires, but what if we were to narrow it down to just one thing. What is my priority in prayer? What is the one thing I would ask of God?

I have bills that need to be payed, sick family members who need a miracle, a family that I want to see blessed, a ministry that I want to grow. I want to see souls saved and revival come to my nation. So many longings. But what is number one? If the King said, ask for one thing and it's yours, what would it be?

The Response

Esther's response to the king's question is remarkable. We all know what she should be asking for - the salvation of the Jews. Her people are about to be annihilated, the king is the only one who can save her and he's just told her that she can ask for anything and it's hers. This is her hero moment - her opportunity to save the people! And yet when she responds to the king she never mentions the salvation of the Jews at all.

> *"'If it pleases the king," replied Esther, "let the king, together with Haman, come today to a banquet I have prepared for him."' (Esther 5:4)*

This is her response to the king's question to ask him for anything - would he come to dinner with her later that evening! What a let-down! Imagine being in the presence of the most powerful person on the planet, being given the opportunity to ask him for anything, and all Esther can think of is to ask that the king would have a meal with her!

Can you imagine the response of Mordecai when he hears about this! He has called the Jews to pray and fast for three days and three nights in the hope that the king would listen to Esther. He has not only done that but he has given her such favour that she can ask him for anything. It seemed like God has heard the cries of the Jews and moved the heart of the king. Esther was perfectly positioned to plead for the salvation of her people. And she blew it! What a waste! What a mistake! Dinner with the king? Are you kidding me?!

That evening Esther and the king sat down for dinner. As they were seated at the table, the king looked at his bride and gave her another golden opportunity:

'So the king and Haman went to the banquet Esther had prepared. As they were drinking wine, the king again asked Esther, "Now what is your petition? It will be given you. And what is your request? Even up to half the kingdom, it will be granted."' (v5-6)

Esther had another chance to save her people. For the second time, the king told her she could ask for anything. Once again she had an opportunity to fall on her knees and beg for the salvation of the Jews. And yet once again she failed to take the opportunity:

'Esther replied, "My petition and my request is this: If the king regards me with favour and if it pleases the king to grant my petition and fulfil my request, let the king and Haman come tomorrow to the banquet I will prepare for them."' (v7-8)

Once again, the only thing Esther asked for is that the king would come to another banquet the following day. What was Esther's problem? Didn't she care about the Jews? Why would she rather have a meal with the king than petition him about the salvation of her people?

The Bride's Choice

Esther knew something that we as the Bride of Christ also have to discover. Discovering this will change our prayer life and the way that we view spiritual warfare. Esther knew that the king craved communion. And Esther knew that if she could satisfy the heart of the king by dining with Him, everything else would take care of itself.

The book of Esther begins with a banquet. Let's go back to chapter one for a moment:

'For a full 180 days he (the king) displayed the vast wealth of his kingdom and the splendour and glory of his majesty. When these days were over, the king gave a banquet, lasting seven days, in the enclosed garden of the king's palace, for all the people from the least to the greatest who were in the citadel of Susa. The garden had hangings of white and blue linen, fastened with cords of white linen and purple material to silver rings on marble pillars. There were couches of gold and silver on a mosaic pavement of porphyry, marble, mother-of-pearl and other costly stones. Wine was served in goblets of gold, each one different from the other, and the royal wine was abundant, in keeping with the king's liberality. By the king's command each guest was allowed to drink without restriction, for the king instructed all the wine stewards to serve each man what he wished.' (Esther 1:4-8)

The Bible is describing the king's banquet. It is one of majesty, splendour, and abundance. There has probably never been a banquet like it, hosted by an earthly king.

How much more glorious is the Banqueting Table of our King? The Table of King Jesus is full of glory and majesty. It contains all that we need and it contains it in abundance. Joy is on the menu. Healing is on the menu. Provision is on the menu. Forgiveness is on the menu. Life itself is on the menu. You can even taste the very presence of the King Himself. What a glorious feast has been prepared for us by our King!

While all of this is taking place, where was Queen Vashti? The Bible tells us that she was having her own banquet. (v9). After a week of feasting, King Xerxes called for his bride. He asked her to leave her banquet and come to his banquet; he wanted communion with his bride, he wanted to eat and drink with his most favoured one.

But Vashti refused. She wanted to continue to do her own thing, enjoying her own banquet and wouldn't leave it for anyone. It didn't matter that the kings banquet was far superior to her own, she was happy dining at her own table, and she refused to come to the king's table.

This decision would cost her her position, title, and influence. It would cost her everything.

The King will always give us a choice: do you want to eat at Vashti's table or the King's table? Do you want to eat from the tree of knowledge or the tree of life? Do you want to eat at your own table or do you want to come to mine?

Vashti's table is good, but it is inferior compared to the king's. Nothing can compare to dining with Him. Nothing compares to communing with Him.

For churches, Vashti's table speaks of dead religion. It speaks of religious gatherings and programmes that contain a form of godliness, but miss out the one vital component that the King longs for - communion, fellowship, intimacy, relationship.

The thing about religion - doing things in God's Name without God's presence - is that we can think that it tastes wonderful. We enjoy our programmes, we enjoy our songs, we enjoy the stuff that we do for Him.

But there is something better that He is calling us to - communion. "Sit with Me." "Dine with Me." "Fellowship with Me."

For two thousand years He has been calling us to, "leave your own banquet and come to My banquet," "leave your religious gatherings and empty ceremonies and sit with Me for a moment. Eat of Me, drink of Me, enjoy Me."

But like Vashti, we have refused. Like Vashti we carry on going through the motions, preparing our own religious banquets, not realising that there is something far greater available. No wonder we have lost our influence in the nation. Our influence and authority only comes due to our relationship with the King. Without that, we are left with nothing.

I don't know if you have ever eaten at a particular restaurant and been certain that it was the best restaurant in town. You have told everyone you meet, "You want to eat somewhere good? - that is the place!" Then one day you meet a friend and they tell you that there is another restaurant across town that is better. You can hardly believe it, but one day you decide to go. As you sit down to eat, you are initially a little unsure, but then the food comes and you take a bite. Even as you swallow that first mouthful, you suddenly realise that your friend was right, this place is better! I can guarantee one thing, you will never go back to that old restaurant. What you thought was the best has suddenly become inferior now that you have tasted that there is something better available.

In the same way once you have tasted and seen that the Lord is good (Psalm 34:8) nothing else will satisfy. You can never go back to dead religion, you can never go back to ceremony and routine - the only thing that will satisfy is the presence of the King.

What is the table that you are eating from? What is the thing that satisfies you? Is it the things of this world? Is it your house, your career, your hobbies? Friends, once you have dined with the King, once you have communed and fellowshipped with Him, once you have tasted of His presence and drunk from His life giving stream, only one thing will satisfy. You are ruined for everything else. I have become predictable in my eating habits. I have become addicted to eating and drinking from the Lord's Table. His presence is all that I want. His presence is all that I need.

Even sin may taste pleasurable for a while, (Hebrews 11:25) but when you have eaten of the hidden Manna and drunk from the new wine of His covenant - you know that only the King's Table can provide you with joy, only the King's Table can give you life, only the King's Table can satisfy you. This is where I go to for nourishment. This is the thing that sustains me. His presence is my very food and drink, and nothing can compare with it.

The King's Desire

Esther was aware of Vashti's choice and decided to make a better one. Esther knew that the desire and longing of the king was to have communion with his bride. This is what he asked of Vashti and she had refused to come to his table. So now, Esther took the initiative, knowing that if she could get the king to the table, if they could just spend time together in communion, she would satisfy his heart. In satisfying his heart, every need she had and that the Jewish people had would get met automatically. That's why she never mentioned her needs or the needs of her people. She knew that if she could meet the king's need then her own needs would get met. Her priority was him. Spending time in his presence.

As we have already looked at so far in this book, the great desire and longing of King Jesus is for communion with His Bride: 'With desire I have desired to eat this Passover with you.' (Luke 22:15 - KJV) He tenderly woos us to His table. His greatest thought, His greatest longing, His greatest desire is to fellowship with us. To eat with us, to drink with us, to spend time with us in communion. This is His greatest joy. This is His greatest passion.

Those that know the heart of the King have discovered this. And they have found this key - if I can satisfy the Kings heart, if I can touch Him by communing with Him, all my needs and all my requests will be met automatically.

The great power of prayer is that we can ask for anything and it will be given to us. But this great blessing can be a great danger as we get so caught up in the "things" that we forget the most important thing of all - fellowshipping with Him.

But those that know the King's heart know that all their needs and wants are secondary - my priority is communion. My priority is being in His presence.

That is why Esther didn't mention the salvation of the Jews. It wasn't because it wasn't important, it was just that it wasn't her priority. Her priority was the king himself.

Jesus put it like this:

'Suppose one of you has a servant ploughing or looking after the sheep. Will he say to the servant when he comes in from the field, "Come along now and sit down to eat?" Won't he rather say, "Prepare my supper, get yourself ready and wait on me while I eat and drink; after that you may eat and drink?"' (Luke 17:7-8)

The principle is this: instead of focusing on getting your needs met, focus on the Master. Make sure that the Master is satisfied before you move onto your own needs. What satisfies the Master? Communion. Spending time with you. That should be our only goal and concern when I come to pray - have I spent time with Jesus? Even in an hour of great crisis like Esther faced, when the clock was ticking and a nation's future hung in the balance, she found time to just spend time, eating and drinking with the king. That is all that matters - Him. His presence. Fellowshipping with Him.

'One thing I ask from the Lord, this only do I seek: that I may dwell in the house of the Lord all the days of my life, to gaze on the beauty of the Lord.' (Psalm 27:4)

'But one thing is needed, and Mary has chosen that good part, which will not be taken away from her.' (Luke 10:42 – NKJV)

'But seek first His kingdom and His righteousness, and all these things will be given to you as well.' (Matthew 6:33)

The Place of Victory

You may have noticed that when Esther invited the king to dinner, she made sure that there were three places at the table - one for her, one for the king and one for Haman. Why Haman? Haman was her enemy. Haman was the one trying to destroy the Jews.

Esther knew that there was only one way Haman could be defeated - to bring him to the table.

Haman was second in command in the most powerful empire on the planet. His plans to annihilate the Jews were already in place, the gallows to hang Mordecai on were already erected. Esther couldn't stop him. It wasn't in her power to change the situation. But she knew - if she could just get him to the table - she knew the king would take care of everything... If I can just get my enemy to the table – I know that everything will be alright.

This revelation truly shows us the power of communion. Surely He has prepared a table for us in the presence of our enemies. (Psalm 23:5) Whatever your enemy is today, whatever it is in your life that is trying to destroy you - bring it to the Table.

For some sin is destroying you. For some an addiction. For some it is fear. For some it is guilt and shame. For others it is a lack of confidence. For others depression or anxiety. Some have an enemy of cancer. Some it is lack. Some it an abusive relationship or a rebellious child. We could go on and on. We all have enemies in our lives, we all have things that the enemy sends to destroy us.

The mistake that many of us make is that we try and fight Haman. You can't fight Haman. You can't defeat sin in your own strength. You can't shake off depression or fear. You can't heal yourself of that incurable disease. But you can bring those things to the Table! You might not have the ability or the power to change things, but the King does. If you can bring those things to His table and allow Him to deal with them, everything will be ok.

Many believers make this mistake when it comes to spiritual warfare. Whether they are praying for the salvation of a loved one or revival to come to a nation, they somehow think that they have to fight for the breakthrough, that they have to make something happen with their wrestling and struggling. Even the greatest prayer warrior on the planet cannot change anyone or anything. But the King can!

One of the greatest intercessors in the Bible is Esther. She literally stood between the living and the dead, between the purposes of God and the powers of hell, and through her influence an entire nation was saved! And what did she do? She sat at a table and had a meal with the king.

The greatest warfare takes place at the Table. The Table is where we fight our battles. We must never take on the enemy and bypass the Table. Here battles are fought, here the victory is won, here the enemy is defeated.

It was here, again as they were sat at the table that the king turned and said for the third time to Queen Esther:

"Queen Esther, what is your petition? It will be given you. What is your request? Even up to half the kingdom, it will be granted." (Esther 7:2)

Esther knows that now is the time. She has dined with the king. His heart had been touched and his needs met. She had brought her enemy to the table. Only now does she know that she can speak and everything will change. She tells the king of the plot to annihilate her people. Stunned by this, the king demands to know who would dare do such a thing.

Queen Esther looked across the table and pointed: 'An adversary and enemy! This vile Haman!' (Esther 7:6)

There is wisdom in coming to the Table and bringing our adversary with us! Not only was she perfectly positioned to speak directly to the king, but her enemy was perfectly positioned to be dealt with by the king himself.

The Bible tells us that at these words "the king got up in a rage," (v7). When we do warfare at the Table something powerful happens - God begins to arise on our behalf. And when God arises His enemies are scattered (Psalm 68:1)

Some of us having been fighting and battling for years and not seen the breakthrough, but if we will just come to the Table then we will find that God will fight for us! The King will deal with every enemy and our victory is assured. We don't need to fight any more - we just need to commune.

Haman's response meanwhile was to try and plead for his life. Haman's power was always in his words. Even then, he reasoned, if he could just come up with the right phrase or the best excuse, maybe his words would save him.

Satan's greatest weapon is also his words. Whether it be words of fear, words of accusation or just plain lies, he is always speaking his words of poison in the ears of God's people.

> *'As soon as the word left the king's mouth,*
> *they covered Haman's face.' (v8)*

As the king came back to the table, Haman's face was covered and he lost his ability to communicate. As he could no longer speak, he no longer had any power. His fate was sealed.

The powerful truth is that satan is silenced at the Table. He is constantly lying, scheming, sowing seeds of doubt and fear, but He has no response to what is on the Table. Show him the Bread. Show him the Wine. He is rendered speechless. He cannot respond. He has nothing to say when confronted with the Bread of His Presence. He has nothing to say when confronted with the Blood of the Lamb. Every fear is swallowed up, every lie is exposed, every accusation is silenced.

As Spurgeon put it "He who fights with the blood of Jesus fights with a weapon which cannot know defeat. The blood of Jesus: sin dies at its presence, death ceases to be death, and heavens gates are opened. The blood of Jesus – we shall march on, conquering and to conquer as long as we trust in its power."

The Turn Around

In coming to the table and bringing her enemy with her, Esther positioned herself to help facilitate one of the greatest miracle stories in the Bible.

Firstly, Haman himself was dealt with. Ironically the same gallows that he built to hang Mordecai on, he himself was hanged upon. If only Haman would have known, perhaps he would never have built those gallows in the first place. Every time he hammered a nail into the gallows, little did he realise he was sealing his own destruction.

The parallel with our great adversary is obvious as he didn't realise as he was crucifying Jesus that he was actually paving the way for his own defeat.
(1 Corinthians 2:8)

It is this defeat of satan that we remind ourselves of and enforce every time we have communion with the King. Whenever we come to the Lord's Table we also show satan his gallows, which is the cross of Calvary. Surely our fear is hung there, our guilt and shame is hung there, our sickness hangs there, even death itself hangs there. The defeat is total, and eternal.

The second thing that happens was that the king proclaimed another decree in response to the one that had already been made at the request of Haman. This is important for us to note. The king did not ignore the first decree. He just made another decree. And this second decree overruled the first.

According to Jesus, the act of Communion is an act of proclamation, "you proclaim the Lord's death until He comes" (1 Corinthians 11:26). What are we proclaiming? We are proclaiming that another decree has been made. Satan may have pronounced death over us, but the King has made another decree, "death is defeated." Satan may have pronounced sickness over us, but the King makes another decree, "by My stripes you are healed." God does not ignore our sins and failures, but in response to the accuser He makes another decree, "My blood cleanses, My blood forgives, My blood washes away, My blood makes you clean, My blood makes you righteous, My blood makes you worthy." Glory to God, that the words of this second decree, the power of this New Covenant are more powerful than the words of the written code that has been nailed to the tree with Him. Those words now no longer have power over us: "All sins forgiven, the slate wiped clean, that old arrest warrant cancelled and nailed to Christ's cross." (Colossians 2:14 - The Mess)

The third thing that takes place is that the King gives the Jews the right to take up arms against their enemies. (Esther 8:11) He empowered them to defeat their enemies and see the victory of God, a victory that is remembered to this day through the feast of Purim. It is significant for us to note that although some enemies were defeated straight away at the table (Haman), other enemies were still out there. But now, the Jews had been empowered to fight back and gain the victory.

When we have communion with Jesus, many of our enemies are defeated immediately and we see sudden breakthroughs, miracles and answers to prayer. But then there are other enemies that seem to hang around a little longer. We leave the Communion Table and it seems like nothing has happened. But there are two ways in which God gives us the victory - He either deals with the enemy directly, or He empowers us to overcome him. Either way, something happens at the Table.

At the table, Xerxes gave the Jews permission to pick up a sword and fight. At the Lord's Table, He anoints our heads with oil (Psalm 23:5) which speaks of the anointing of the Holy Spirit. As I commune with the King, I am empowered by the Spirit of God and I leave His presence with an authority and an ability to defeat and overcome all the powers of hell, "I have given you authority…to overcome all the power of the enemy; nothing will harm you." (Luke 10:19)

In a remarkable chain of events the book of Esther reveals that "the tables were turned and the Jews got the upper hand over those who hated them." (9:1) This is what God is able to do!

I believe even reading this that there are people and it seems like the enemy is about to defeat you. It seems like your situation is hopeless and there is nothing you can do. But in a moment God can turn the tables! In a moment He can change the whole situation around for His glory. He is the God of the turnaround, the God who always wins and always leads His people into victory. (2 Corinthians 2:14)

What a lesson we can learn from the life of Esther. Despite the circumstances, focus on the King. Focus on touching His heart. Come to His Table. Dine with Him. Fellowship with Him. In doing so you are positioning yourself for a miracle and placing yourself where you can be empowered by His Spirit. Bring your enemy to the Table with you and leave him there. He is silenced at the Table, He is defeated at the Table. He is the turnaround God, watch Him turn things around for you!

A Prayer of Response

"Precious Jesus, You are my one thing. Although I have many desires, my greatest desire is for You. Although I have many needs, my greatest need is You. My one request, my one petition is to spend time in communion with You. God, you see my enemies. I cannot defeat them in my own strength so I bring them into Your presence. I bring every fear, every sickness, every sin and I place them at Your Table, in Your Presence. Oh, God arise on my behalf! Fight for me and scatter every enemy. Proclaim Your Words that silence every enemy. Empower me with Your Spirit with the authority and power that I need to enforce Your victory. Amen."

"The flesh feeds on the body and blood of Christ that the soul may likewise be filled with God."

- *Tertullian*

10
A NEW ORDER

"You are a priest forever, in the order of Melchizedek."

(Hebrews 5:6)

In this chapter we are going to look in some detail at one of the most precious offices that Jesus holds. He is our God, our Saviour, our Lord, our Friend, our Bridegroom. He is so many things to us. But He is also our great High Priest. The book of Hebrews devotes several verses to discussing the role of Jesus as our Priest.

'Therefore, since we have a great High Priest who has ascended into Heaven, Jesus the Son of God, let us hold firmly to the faith we profess. For we do not have a high priest who is unable to feel sympathy for our weaknesses, but we have one who has been tempted in every way, just as we are – yet He did not sin. Let us then approach God's throne of grace with confidence, so that we may receive mercy and find grace to help us in our time of need.' (Hebrews 4:14-16)

The role of the priest was key in the life of Jewish worship. From the time of Aaron and the commencement of the Levitical priesthood, thousands of men had served as priests, standing in the gap between men and God. They had come, they had served, and they had died. But then came the Great High Priest. The greatest High Priest of them all. Unlike previous high priests who died, this Priest lives forever, and therefore has a "permanent priesthood." Therefore He 'always lives to make intercession' for us. (Hebrews 7:23-25)

Our Intercessor

The picture that the book of Hebrews paints is of a priest who is kind, good and sympathetic. He knows what it is to be tempted by sin. He knows what it is to feel weakness. And yet He overcame sin, He overcame weakness. He was perfect, spotless, totally without sin. So on the one hand He has power and on the other hand He has mercy. He is therefore the perfect priest to act as our intercessor, bringing our needs before His Father.

Exodus 28 gives us a detailed description of the garments that the high priest would wear. Verses 11-12 show how the priest would take precious stones engraved with the names of the sons of Israel and he would wear them upon his shoulders when he went into the presence of God. This is a wonderful picture of how our Great High Priest, Jesus, takes our burdens upon His shoulders and brings them into the presence of the Father.

All of us have burdens, fears, worries and concerns. Sometimes we feel that we have to carry them. We go through life weighed down by stress and pressure, and lose our sense of joy and peace. But if we could only see that we have a High Priest who will carry our burdens for us: 'Praise be to the Lord, to God our Saviour, who daily bear our burdens.' (Psalm 68:19) Bring your burdens to Jesus! Bring your needs, worries, and cares to your wonderful High Priest. He will carry them for you. He will even carry you if you let Him! We are weak and powerless - but He is mighty, He is strong, He is able.

Exodus 28 goes on to tell us that the High Priest would also 'Bear the names of the sons of Israel over his heart.' How precious this is. Not only does He carry your burdens, but He holds you close to His heart. Right now you are on the mind of Jesus. Right now you are on His heart. If you were to look at the prayer list of Jesus, your name would be right at the top! He knows you. He knows your name. He knows your needs. He knows your worries, doubts and fears. And He is praying for you! He is interceding for you! He is bringing your name before His Father.

Robert Murray McCheyne put it powerfully:

'If I could hear Christ praying for me in the next room, I would not fear a million enemies. Yet distance makes no difference. He is praying for me.'

The Levitical Priesthood

The vast majority of the Old Testament verses that speak of the priesthood are referring to the Levitical priesthood. Aaron, the brother of Moses was Israel's first high priest, and after him, it was his descendants; those from the tribe of Levi that were appointed priests.

Because there are so many verses in the Bible referring to the Levitical priesthood, for many of us that is our point of reference when we think of the role of a priest. However, the book of Hebrews makes it very clear that the role of Jesus as our High Priest is not like the Levitical priests that served in the Tabernacle and the Temple. Jesus came as a different kind of high priest, one of the order of the mysterious Melchizedek.

The Levitical priesthood was undoubtedly a blessing for Israel in that time, but in many ways the Old Testament priests was powerless to truly meet the needs of the people.

This is why Hebrews tells us that there was a 'still a need for another priest to come.' (Hebrews 7:11)

The Levitical priesthood could only cover sin, but it could never totally forgive, wipe out, and wash away sin. The Levitical priesthood could atone for sin each year but then another sacrifice would have to be made. There was no permanent sacrifice that would do away with sin forever. The Levitical priests could pronounce over people that their sins and previous wrong doings had been covered, but they had no ability to impart into people the power to overcome the sinful nature itself.

The Levitical priesthood was not able to bring people into a place of perfection, (Hebrews 7:11) meaning wholeness or completeness. The people were not truly able to be reconciled to God. It was a partial ministry of redemption.

The Greatest High Priest

Because the Levitical priesthood was in many ways weak and useless, God had to give us another High Priest; Jesus, who would be very different to the Old Testament Levitical priests. Jesus would come with a better hope and a better covenant, because He is a better Priest; one who has been chosen not on the basis of His ancestry but 'on the basis of the power of an indestructible life.' (Hebrews 7:15)

Everything that the Levitical priesthood was unable to do, Jesus is able to do. He deals with sin forever. He removes sin forever. He washes away sin forever.

Chapter 10 of Hebrews puts it like this:

'Day after day every priest stands and performs his religious duties; again and again he offers the same sacrifices, which can never take away sins. But when this priest had offered for all time one sacrifice for sins, He sat down at the right hand of God, and since that time He waits for his enemies to be made his footstool. For by one

sacrifice He has made perfect forever those who are being made holy.' (v11-14)

Let's read this again but in the New King James version:

'And every priest stands ministering daily and offering repeatedly the same sacrifices, which can never take away sins. But this Man, after He had offered one sacrifice for sins forever, sat down at the right hand of God, from that time waiting till His enemies are made His footstool. For by one offering He has perfected forever those who are being sanctified.'

And now one more time, but now in the Amplified Bible:

'Every priest stands [at his altar of service] ministering daily, offering the same sacrifices over and over, which are never able to strip away sins [that envelop and cover us]; whereas Christ, having offered the one sacrifice [the all-sufficient sacrifice of Himself] for sins for all time, sat down [signifying the completion of atonement for sin] at the right hand of God [the position of honour], waiting from that time onward until His enemies are made a footstool for His feet. For by the one offering He has perfected forever and completely cleansed those who are being sanctified [bringing each believer to spiritual completion and maturity].'

It was a one-time sacrifice and that was enough. He dealt with our sin once and for all on the cross. His sacrifice enables us to be made perfect - in other words, it makes us whole, complete. He has given us perfect redemption, a perfect salvation. It is not temporary, it doesn't need to be assessed on an annual basis - it is forever 'He became the source of eternal salvation.' (Hebrews 5:9)

This High Priest has not only removed our sins forever but He has also given us the power to overcome sin by writing his laws on our minds and hearts. (Hebrews 8:10)

Whereas under the Levitical priesthood, mankind was kept at a distance with the only the high priest himself being allowed into the Most Holy Place, our Great High Priest has made a way for all of us to enter through the veil. (Hebrews 6:19) We can all draw near to God (Hebrews 7:19) and enjoy a close fellowship with Him. Every one of us can come before His throne with confidence so that we can 'receive mercy and find grace to help us in our time of need.' (Hebrews 4:16). Jesus, our Great High Priest has made a way.

'Our time of need' - whenever that is, He has made a way. We can come anytime into His presence. We can receive. We can find. Help, mercy, grace, it is all available in Jesus.

'Such a High Priest meets our needs.' (Hebrews 7:26) Whatever that need is today - Jesus is able to meet it. (v25) Do we need forgiveness? Do we need strength? Do we need the power to overcome? Do we need healing? Do we need to be made whole? Jesus, our Great High Priest is willing and able to meet every need!

Who is Melchizedek?

Hebrews makes it very clear that all of these incredible things that Jesus did for us were not available under the Levitical priesthood. That is why He had to come as a different high priest - not one like Aaron, but one like Melchizedek.

Several times in the book of Hebrews it stresses: Jesus is not like Aaron, if you approach him like the children of Israel approached Aaron you will never receive all the benefits of this perfect salvation. You must see Jesus like Melchizedek. You must approach him like Melchizedek.

Although Melchizedek is referenced in a couple of places in Scripture, he only appears personally in one place - Genesis 14. Let's read about him:

'After Abram returned from defeating Kedorlaomer and the kings allied with him, the king of Sodom came out to meet him in the Valley of Shaveh (that is, the King's Valley).

Then Melchizedek king of Salem brought out bread and wine. He was priest of God Most High, and he blessed Abram, saying,

"Blessed be Abram by God Most High, Creator of heaven and earth. And praise be to God Most High, who delivered your enemies into your hand."

Then Abram gave him a tenth of everything.' (v18-20)

Melchizedek only appears in these three verses and yet Hebrews tells us that these verses show us what Jesus, our Great High Priest is like.

Melchizedek is what we would call a prophetic type of the Lord Jesus. Like Jesus, Melchizedek is both a king and a priest (the only two individuals in scripture of whom this is so). Melchizedek's name means the "king of righteousness," and he is the king of Salem (Jerusalem) which means "peace." He is the king of righteousness and the king of peace.

Our High Priest, Jesus, is not only our Priest, but He is also King. Indeed He is the King above all kings, just like He is the Priest above all priests. He is the Righteous King, the Prince of Peace, the One who is pure, holy, awesome, and glorious. He is 'Holy, blameless, pure, set apart from sinners, exalted above the heavens.' (Hebrews 7:26)

Abram's encounter with Melchizedek may be brief, but it is significant. Putting all these scriptures together that we have looked at and tying them up with the Genesis 14 story changes the way we approach our High Priest.

When Melchizedek met Abram, he only did two things. Firstly, he gave him bread and wine - symbols of communion and covenant. They had a communion meal together. This is the first time the bread and wine are mentioned in connection with a meal. This is also the first time the priesthood is mentioned. The second thing that happens is that after the bread and wine have been given, Abram is blessed by the priest.

Remember, Jesus is not a high priest like Levi, He is a high priest like Melchizedek.

What happened under the Levitical priesthood? Under the Levitical priesthood the people would bring their sacrifice and their offering to the priest. What was the prerequisite? The sacrifice had to be pure, without spot or blemish. The priest would examine the sacrifice looking for fault, looking for imperfections. If he found anything wrong, the people were sent anyway. Only if it was a perfect offering could he then pronounce a blessing over the people.

But what happened under Melchizedek? Under Melchizedek there was no examination of Abram's offering. Why? Because Abram didn't bring one. In a total turn around, it was the priest himself who brought the gift - he brought the bread and wine. All Abram had to do was sit down, and eat, drink, and fellowship with the priest. Then what happened? He got blessed! Melchizedek blessed Abram without requiring anything from him - other than communion.

Please see this picture. Under Levi, you give the priest your best, and if it's good enough, you receive a blessing. Under Melchizedek you don't bring anything to him. He comes to you. He gives to you. He blesses you. All you do, is receive the bread and wine that he offers.

Isn't this what Jesus said He would do: 'It will be good for those servants whose master finds them watching when he comes. Truly I tell you, he will dress himself to serve, will make them recline at the table and will come and wait on them.' (Luke 12:37)

Which Priesthood Do You Choose?

Although all believers would recognise Jesus as their High Priest, many of us still think that He is a priest like Aaron. This is not the case. How many of us still think that what God requires of us is to bring our best to Him. We bring Him our prayers, our worship, our money, our time, our service, our righteousness.

We then subconsciously think of Jesus as our priest inspecting what we give Him. We somehow think that if only what we give is perfect then we may obtain His blessing.

How many of us have wondered 'Is my prayer life good enough?' 'Is my worship acceptable?' 'Am I giving enough?' 'Am I spending enough time with God?' 'Is God pleased with me?'

We are continually hoping that our best is enough, forever wondering if we are good enough for God to bless us. We are striving to be better Christians, continually aiming for perfection.

This is what it is like to see Jesus as Aaron/Levi. But He isn't. Hebrews tells us that seeing Jesus like this leads to a faith that is weak and useless. (Hebrews 7:19) But we don't have to live like this! There has been a change of priesthood (Hebrews 7:12) and the old priesthood has been set aside.

He is my Melchizedek. He comes to me, and He offers me bread and wine. He doesn't demand that I bring anything to Him, after all even my best is not good enough. My best prayer is not good enough. Whatever I give Him could never be enough. My own righteousness is like filthy rags in His sight. And it is in seeing this that freedom is found. I don't have to strive, I don't have to try harder. I just have to receive. I just have to believe. I just have to rest and trust Him.

He is not looking for my imperfections - He already knows them. Instead He is offering me His perfect sacrifice - symbolised in the Bread and Wine; and He is saying, "receive this" "eat and drink this" "trust that this meal is enough for you to receive my blessing" "I don't want you to try, I want you to trust."

Melchizedek did not require anything from Abram other than time spent in communion. That was enough for him to speak a blessing over him - and Abram was blessed!

Our blessing is even greater than the blessing Abram received. Our Great High Priest has blessed us in the Heavenly realms with every spiritual blessing in Christ. (Ephesians 1:3) Every blessing is ours. But notice the key - in Christ. Not in me somehow attaining a level of perfection - but in me abiding in Christ. Trusting in His sacrifice, recognising that that is enough and that all things have been 'freely given us in the One he loves.' (v6)

The reason that this Priesthood is perfect is because this Priest is perfect:
- His works are perfect (Deuteronomy 32)
- His ways are perfect (2 Samuel 22)

- His knowledge is perfect (Job 36)
- His word is perfect (Psalm 19)
- His faithfulness is perfect (Isaiah 25)
- His peace is perfect (Isaiah 26)
- His will is perfect (Romans 12)
- His unity is perfect (1 Corinthians 1)
- His power is perfect (2 Corinthians 12)
- His gifts are perfect (James 1)
- His love is perfect (1 John 4)

He is the perfect High Priest, and the perfect Saviour. His sacrifice is perfect.

Under Levi, you bring your best to God and you are still not perfect, so you try harder, you strive more, but you will never achieve perfection.

But under Melchizedek, you eat the bread and you are eating perfection. You drink the cup and you are drinking perfection. You are dining with a perfect High Priest, receiving His perfect life and trusting in His perfect sacrifice.

You are what you eat. As you receive the Bread and Wine, as you commune with Him and trust that what He did was enough, He makes you perfect. His perfect life is imparted into you. He makes you worthy, makes you righteous, makes you whole and complete. He does it all. All you do is receive.

I cannot stress how important it is for us to see that no longer do you need to bring your gift to the altar to be inspected by Levi. The call of the New Testament is no longer 'come to the altar' but 'come to the table.'
He is calling us to come and dine with Him. Trust in His finished work and look to that as our life source.

> *'When this Priest had offered for all time one sacrifice for sins,*
> *He sat down at the right hand of God.' (Hebrews 10:12)*

Religion stands, but faith sits. We are able to sit with Him at the table and trust that when He said "it is finished," He really meant it. After all, it is He that is the perfecter of our faith. (Hebrews 12:2)

Of course, Abram would go on to give to Melchizedek a tenth of all that he had, but this was not to receive the blessing, it was a response to the fact that he had already been blessed! Likewise, the giving of our lives in worship to God is our response to the reality that we have already been blessed. We already have been given all things in Him.

As you come to the Table - see the Bread, see the Wine. See the love. See the sacrifice. Trust in it. Trust in the Body. Trust in the Blood. They are enough. He is enough. Christ is always enough.

> *'Every priest goes to work at the altar each day, offers the same old sacrifices year in, year out, and never makes a dent in the sin problem. As a priest, Christ made a single sacrifice for sins, and that was it! Then He sat down right beside God and waited for His enemies to cave in. It was a perfect sacrifice by a perfect person to perfect some very imperfect people. By that single offering, He did everything that needed to be done for everyone who takes part in the purifying process. The Holy Spirit confirms this:*
>
> *This new plan I'm making with Israel*
> *isn't going to be written on paper,*
> *isn't going to be chiseled in stone;*

*This time "I'm writing out the plan in them,
carving it on the lining of their hearts."*

*He concludes,
I'll forever wipe the slate clean of their sins.
Once sins are taken care of for good, there's no longer
any need to offer sacrifices for them.'*

(Hebrews 10:13-18 – The Mess)

A Prayer of Response

"Oh Lord Jesus, how wonderful it is to acknowledge You as my High Priest. Even now I am on Your heart. Even now You are thinking of me. Even now You are praying for me. Jesus, I sit here in my weakness and my imperfections, but right here, just as I am, You come to me. You come offering your Body and Your Blood. You come inviting me to dine with You. Oh Jesus, I respond to Your invitation. I sit with You and I dine with You. I receive Your perfect life and perfect love. I trust in Your finished work, I trust in Your sacrifice. Oh Jesus You have blessed me in every way! In You I am blessed. In You I am whole. In You I am complete. Oh Jesus, my response is to worship You, to give You my life, to give You my all, to tell You how much I love You. Amen."

"O most admirable banquet, to which it is an unspeakable favour to be invited! There is no language adequate to describe the joy one experiences through this sacrament which draws sweetness from its very source and keeps alive in us the memory of love, of which Christ gave proof during His passion."

- St. Thomas Aquinas

11

SHADOWS OF THE CHRIST

"These are a shadow of the things that were to come; the reality, however, is found in Christ."

(Colossians 2:17)

As well as believing that the Old Testament is full of literal, historically accurate events, I also am a strong believer in the prophetic typology of the Old Testament in relationship to the person of Jesus. Typology in Christian theology and Biblical exegesis is a doctrine or theory concerning the relationship of the Old Testament to the New Testament. Events, persons, or statements in the Old Testament are seen as types or shadows pre-figuring or superseded by antitypes, events or aspects of Christ or His revelation described in the New Testament.

One of the clearest and most obvious prophetic types in the Old Testament is the prophet Jonah. Jesus Himself indicated that Jonah was a prophetic type in Matthew 12 where He describes Jonah being in the belly of the fish for three days and three nights as a direct foreshadowing of His own death, burial, and resurrection.

In this chapter we will look at two more prophetic types of Jesus and how the story of the Communion Table plays a part in their narrative.

Joseph

One character from the Old Testament that is often seeing as a type of Christ is Joseph, whose story is found in Genesis 37-50.

There are many ways in which Joseph could be seen as a prophetic foreshadowing of Jesus, but some of the most obvious are:

- They were both rejected by their own people.
- They were both betrayed for silver.
- They were both falsely accused.
- They were both situated at the right hand of their respective thrones.
- They were both 30 years of age when they came into places of influence.
- They both brought salvation to the world (one physical, one spiritual).
- As Joseph married an Egyptian bride, so Jesus would include the Gentiles in His Bride, the Church.

There are other comparisons that we can make between Joseph and Jesus but what I find fascinating in the context of this book is the prophetic symbolism of the bread and wine, and the banqueting table that are found throughout the life of Joseph.

Restoration, Exchange, and Destiny

The first time that we see the prophetic imagery of the Communion meal is when we see Joseph in prison after being falsely accused by the wife of Potiphar.

Whilst in prison Joseph encounters two men who share with him their dreams:

> 'Some time later, the cupbearer and the baker of the king of Egypt offended their master, the king of Egypt. Pharaoh was angry with his two officials, the chief

cupbearer and the chief baker, and put them in custody in the house of the captain of the guard, in the same prison where Joseph was confined. The captain of the guard assigned them to Joseph, and he attended them.
After they had been in custody for some time, each of the two men - the cupbearer and the baker of the king of Egypt, who were being held in prison - had a dream the same night, and each dream had a meaning of its own.' (Genesis 40:1-5)

When you read this story through the lens of looking for shadows and types of the Lord's Table, the imagery suddenly becomes obvious. What does a baker do? Make bread. What did a cupbearer do? Deliver wine. So right here in these two men we see a picture of the Bread and Wine.

And how did God use these two men? The butler and the baker became the men that God would use to release Joseph into his destiny. The bread and wine became the methods that God used to transport Joseph from the prison to the palace, and from a place of captivity into a place of power. From a place of hopelessness, the bread and the wine ushered Joseph into the fulfilment of prophecy. It was the testimony of the bread and the wine that brought Joseph into the presence of Pharaoh. (Genesis 41:9-14)

Here we see the power of the Bread and Wine in our stories too. What the Bread and Wine represent are what God uses to bring us into freedom and purpose. The Bread and Wine give us hope. It is our engagement with the Bread and Wine that help launch each of us into our God given destinies.

The Bread and Wine have a language and a voice. Even though the baker died in Genesis 40, his testimony of Joseph still spoke to Pharaoh in the following chapter. The cupbearer, who did not die but was restored back to Pharaoh's presence, he was the one who speaks on behalf of Joseph to Pharaoh.

The Bread and Wine still speak today. Even though the body of Christ was broken two thousand years ago, His sacrifice still speaks, His wounds still speak. They still speak of our salvation, they still speak of our healing. Even now in the presence of God our King, the blood of Christ is still speaking on our behalf. There is still life in His blood, His blood still speaks. It speaks to God for us and enables us to be brought into the throne room of Heaven and the presence of the King of kings. We have access because the blood testifies on our behalf. It speaks of mercy, grace, and acceptance.

When we study the dreams of the baker and the butler we find more prophetic imagery:

'So the chief cupbearer told Joseph his dream. He said to him, "In my dream I saw a vine in front of me, and on the vine were three branches. As soon as it budded, it blossomed, and its clusters ripened into grapes. Pharaoh's cup was in my hand, and I took the grapes, squeezed them into Pharaoh's cup and put the cup in his hand."

"This is what it means," Joseph said to him. "The three branches are three days. Within three days Pharaoh will lift up your head and restore you to your position, and you will put Pharaoh's cup in his hand, just as you used to do when you were his cupbearer. But when all goes well with you, remember me and show me kindness; mention me to Pharaoh and get me out of this prison. I was forcibly carried off from the land of the Hebrews, and even here I have done nothing to deserve being put in a dungeon."

When the chief baker saw that Joseph had given a favourable interpretation, he said to Joseph, "I too had a dream: on my head were three baskets of bread. In the top basket were all kinds of baked goods for Pharaoh, but the birds were eating them out of the basket on my head."

"This is what it means," Joseph said. "The three baskets are three days. Within three days Pharaoh will lift off your head and impale your body on a pole. And the birds will eat away your flesh."' (Genesis 40:9-19)

Notice the clear prophetic typology here - after three days one person, the baker, symbolised as a bread basket, is hung on a tree and dies. After three days, the cupbearer, symbolised as grapes is restored back to his original position and place.

Three days - the exact amount of time in which Jesus died and rose again. Three days. The baker and the cupbearer. The bread and wine.

In three days the baker - the bread - was hung on a tree. He died but the other man lived. The other man was restored. There was redemption for him - grace, mercy, and forgiveness. Once again he had purpose, once again he was allowed access into Pharaoh's presence.

Here we see the great divine exchange of the cross. One man, the Bread of Life, was hung on a tree. Now the many find redemption, the many find grace, mercy and forgiveness. One man died but now the many find purpose. The many have been restored back into the presence of God.

The great exchange that took place at the cross:

He was punished - we are forgiven
He was wounded - we are healed
He was made sin - we are made righteous
He tasted death - we have eternal life
He was made poor - we share His abundance
He was rejected - we are accepted

He was forsaken - we are adopted
He wore a crown of thorns - we share a Kingdom of Light
He was found guilty - we can walk in freedom
He took the wrath of God - we receive the peace of God
Our rebellion came on Jesus - His goodness comes on us
He was made a curse - we receive the blessing

This part of the story ends with these words: 'he restored the chief cupbearer to his position, so that he once again put the cup into Pharaoh's hand.' (Genesis 40:21)

Surely, God uses our Joseph to restore us back into the presence of God, to restore back to us the divine image and mandate that was lost by Adam. Life eternal has been restored back to us.

Genesis 40 is a story of exchange. A story of death. Of life. Of redemption. Of restoration. Of divine destiny. It is a story of bread and wine. For the Bread and Wine are the instruments that God always uses to bring life and redemption; to restore us, and to release us.

The Bread

As the story of Joseph moves on, we see in Genesis 41-42 that there is a clear focus on the bread.

Pharaoh has a dream about grain (the bread) and the interpretation through Joseph is that a great famine is coming. The fulfilment of this prophecy is found in Genesis 41:53 where it indicates that the famine spread throughout the known world.

But not in Egypt. Egypt has a saviour called Joseph. And Joseph has made sure that there is plenty of bread in Egypt. The storehouses of Egypt are full of grain. While the rest of the world starves, Egypt has an abundance of bread.

Now the nations have a choice. They can continue to die in their famine or they can come to Joseph and buy bread. Joseph is their only hope. He is the only one who can give life when all around them is death.

The parallel here should be obvious. This world is in famine. There is no life in this world. For all our riches, entertainments, and freedoms, we are still starving for hope, joy, love, purpose, and for true freedom. This world cannot give life. This world can only ever produce death.

But we have a Joseph, a Deliver, a Saviour, and His Name is Jesus. He is the Bread of Life. He is able to satisfy every longing and need of the human heart. He is able to fill the emptiness within. In Him is life eternal and abundant. In Him is found an escape from death itself.

The storehouses of heaven are full. They are never empty. They are always full, and overflowing. There is always an abundance of bread on His Table. Whatever we need to satisfy us, whatever is the answer to our need - Jesus has the key to it all.

The nations today still have a choice. You and I have a choice. Do we continue to die in our sin? Do we continue to starve surrounded by barrenness? Or do we come to Jesus? Do we come to our Saviour? Do we receive His life giving bread, His life giving presence? Do we allow Jesus to feed us? Do we allow Jesus to meet every need and fill every empty part? Do we look to Jesus as our source and our salvation? One group of people that came to Joseph were his brothers. Although they did not recognise him, they ended up buying grain from their younger brother. In Genesis 42, they return home, only to find something shocking on their journey:

'Joseph gave orders to fill their bags with grain, to put each man's silver back in his sack, and to give them provisions for their journey. After this was done for them, they loaded their grain on their donkeys and left.

At the place where they stopped for the night one of them opened his sack to get feed for his donkey, and he saw his silver in the mouth of his sack. "My silver has been returned," he said to his brothers. "Here it is in my sack."

Their hearts sank and they turned to each other trembling and said, "What is this that God has done to us?"' (Genesis 42:25-28)

In opening their bags, the brothers discover that the silver that they thought they had used to pay for the grain was right there in the mouths of their sacks. The silver was in the grain. The silver is always in the grain.

In the Bible, silver speaks of redemption and salvation. God was showing them that this was where their deliverance was found, in the grain that comes from Joseph. God is showing us that there is only once place that hope is found - the bread of His Presence.

The reason that the brothers are so afraid is because they think Joseph will accuse them of stealing from him. They had intended to pay for the bread but their money has been returned.

This was entirely deliberate on the part of Joseph. He would not allow them to pay for the bread. He wanted to give it to them for free.

In the same way, we cannot buy or earn the saving bread of Jesus. His grace is entirely free. No good deeds or no observance of the law can save us. We are not saved by our own righteousness. There is nothing that we can give to God to earn or receive His salvation. It is entirely 'by grace you have been saved, through faith - and this is not from yourselves, it is the gift of God, not by works, so that no one can boast.' (Ephesians 2:8-9)

The Table

As Genesis 42 focuses on the grain (the bread), the focus in Genesis 43 is on the table. Here again we see clear prophetic imagery.

Let us remind ourselves for a moment of the complicated relationship Joseph has with his brothers. From his teenage years, these men have been filled with jealousy towards him. They have hated him and despised him, and even plotted to kill him. In the end they have sold him into slavery, and have been responsible for him being separated from his homeland and his beloved father.

These men should be Joseph's enemies. He is now in a position of authority and influence over them. At the very least he could use his power over them to hurt or humiliate them. He could certainly have them thrown into prison. He could even have had them killed. This would be revenge. Some would even see this as justice.

So how does Joseph treat his brothers when they return to Egypt for the second time?

'The steward took the men into Joseph's house, gave them water to wash their feet and provided fodder for their donkeys. They prepared their gifts for Joseph's arrival at noon, because they had heard that they were to eat there.' (Genesis 43:24-25)

How does Joseph treat his enemies? He washes their feet and invites them to dine with him.

This is a clear foreshadowing of Jesus who washed His disciple's feet and then dined with them at the Last Supper. (John 13) Even Judas was among those who had his feet washed and sat at the table with Jesus.

Here we see the amazing grace of our Lord. Even though our sins have put us at enmity with God, even though we have rejected Him and rebelled against Him so many times, even though it was our transgressions that nailed Him to the Cross - still He shows mercy.

Our humble King still stoops down to wash our feet and cleanse us of all unrighteousness. Still He invites us to sit and dine with Him. This is amazing grace. This is remarkable mercy. We deserve so little, and yet we get so much.

Verse 43 of Genesis 43 shows us that the brothers were given to eat food from Joseph's own table. They were not given second best but were allowed to eat the very best that Egypt had to offer. It is the Lord's Table that we eat from. It is His Body we feast on, it is His Blood we drink. We receive His life. We sit in His Presence. The very best that Heaven has to offer is available to us.

As they took their seats at the table the brothers are shocked by the seating arrangements:
'The men had been seated before him in the order of their ages, from the firstborn to the youngest; and they looked at each other in astonishment.' (v33)
It was almost as if this young ruler of the Egyptians knew them. Oh, surely our Lord knows us. He knows not only our age but even the very number of hairs that are on our heads. He knows each of us by name. He knows the plans He has for us. He knows our fears, our longings, and the desires of our heart.

Surely it as at the Table, as we are communing with Him that we discover that each of us are 'fully known.' (1 Corinthians 13:12)

The Wine

As we move on in the story of Joseph we come to Genesis 44, and the completion of our communion typology. As chapter 40 focuses on the bread and wine, chapter 41-42 focus on the grain (the bread), and chapter 43 focuses on the table, chapter 44 focuses fully on the cup (the wine).

Although Joseph shares the same father with his brothers, they have different mothers except Benjamin. Joseph and Benjamin share a special bond as they have the same father and the same mother.

We already see this connection in the previous chapter as Joseph speaks words of grace to Benjamin (Genesis 43:29), and gives him five times as much to eat as the others at the table (Genesis 43:34), five being the prophetic number of grace.

In chapter 44, the brothers return home for the second time only to make another horrific discovery on their way back. In chapter 42 Joseph had placed the brother's silver in their grain sacks, now he puts the cup that he drinks wine from in Benjamin's sack.

At the sight of the cup the brothers are horrified. They fear that Joseph will accuse Benjamin of stealing, and as far as they are concerned the cup will lead to certain judgement and punishment. The cup is bound to lead to imprisonment and death, certainly of Benjamin, but possibly of them all.

Here we see Joseph's masterplan at work. Far from it being a sign of his anger, the cup was the very thing that Joseph would use to get the brother's back into his presence. And it was here, as they returned the third time that Joseph revealed himself to them. It was here that the veil was removed and they were reunited with their brother. It was here that he embraced and kissed them.

The cup that they had been so fearful of, ended up resulting not in judgement but in forgiveness and reconciliation.

The imagery of the cup is one that is used throughout the Bible and it is nearly always referring to the judgement and wrath of God. Isaiah 51 is a typical example of the metaphor of the cup and its link with God's punishment of sin:

> *'Rise up, Jerusalem, you who have drunk from the hand of the Lord the cup of His wrath.' (v17)*

The Bible is very clear - God hates sin and God must punish sin. But at the Lord's Table, Jesus does something remarkable:

> *'The cup of blessing which we bless, is it not the communion of the blood of Christ?' (1 Corinthians 10:16 - NKJV).*

The cup of wrath has become a cup of blessing. The symbolism has changed. Now when Jesus offers us the cup to drink from He is no longer pouring out His judgement, but He is offering us His embrace and His kiss. The cup now for us is no longer used for judgement, because Jesus drunk the cup of judgement Himself. (Luke 22:42) Now the cup is what God uses to bring us back into His presence. The cup is what God uses to forgive, to redeem, to restore, and to reconcile. For the cup is filled with the wine of His blood, 'poured out for many for the forgiveness of sins.'

(Matthew 26:28)

David

As we leave behind the life of Joseph we are going to move on and look at another character from the Old Testament - one who is clearly a prophetic type of the Lord Jesus, one from whom Jesus is a descendant - King David.

There is a story in particular in the life of David that is a beautiful picture of our communion experience with the Lord.

It is actually a story that is referenced by Jesus in all three of the synoptic gospels - Matthew, Mark, and Luke.

'David went to Nob, to Ahimelech the priest. Ahimelech trembled when he met him, and asked, "Why are you alone? Why is no one with you?"

David answered Ahimelech the priest, "The king sent me on a mission and said to me, 'No one is to know anything about the mission I am sending you on.' As for my men, I have told them to meet me at a certain place. Now then, what have you to hand? Give me five loaves of bread, or whatever you can find."

But the priest answered David, "I don't have any ordinary bread to hand; however, there is some consecrated bread here - provided the men have kept themselves from women."
David replied, "Indeed women have been kept from us, as usual whenever I set out. The men's bodies are holy even on missions that are not holy. How much more so today!" So the priest gave him the consecrated bread, since there was no bread there except the bread of the Presence that had been removed from before the Lord

and replaced by hot bread on the day it was taken away.

Now one of Saul's servants was there that day, detained before the Lord; he was Doeg the Edomite, Saul's chief shepherd.

David asked Ahimelech, "Don't you have a spear or sword here? I haven't brought my sword or any other weapon, because the king's mission was urgent."

The priest replied, "The sword of Goliath the Philistine, whom you killed in the Valley of Elah, is here; it is wrapped in a cloth behind the ephod. If you want it, take it; there is no sword here but that one."

David said, "There is none like it; give it to me."'
(1 Samuel 21:1-9)

This time in David's life is one of incredible frustration and pain. Although he has been anointed king, he is not yet on the throne. He is living in that horrible place that we all find ourselves in from time to time - the place in-between the word being spoken and the word being fulfilled. The place of waiting for the promise to manifest. David has been attacked by his father in law Saul, and no doubt feels betrayed and hurt. He is being hunted and fearing for his very life. He has had to flee and leave behind his family, his home, his wife, and his best friend Jonathan.

David is lost, afraid, confused, exhausted, and weary. It seems like he has never been further away from his destiny.
One thing I love about the Bible is that even its greatest heroes have bad days! The feelings of betrayal, fear, exhaustion, loneliness, and of wondering how God's plan fits into my circumstances - we have all been there.

In the midst of this where can David go? Where does he run to? To the priests house! Thank God that when we are feeling weary, exhausted, afraid, and alone there is somewhere we can go to - the presence of our High Priest.

'Therefore, since we have a Great High Priest who has ascended into heaven, Jesus the Son of God, let us hold firmly to the faith we profess. For we do not have a high priest who is unable to feel sympathy for our weaknesses, but we have One who has been tempted in every way, just as we are - yet He did not sin. Let us then approach God's throne of grace with confidence, so that we may receive mercy and find grace to help us in our time of need.' (Hebrews 4:14-15)

Our High Priest is always available and always accessible. When we are living in frustration - go to the High Priest. When we have been hurt - go to the High Priest. When we are confused, lost, fearful, and alone - go to the High Priest. When we are weary and exhausted - go to the High Priest.

The name Ahimelech means 'my brother is the King.' How glorious is Jesus! He is truly all that we need. He is our King. He is our Priest. And He is our brother.

'Both the One who makes people holy and those who are made holy are of the same family. So Jesus is not ashamed to call them brothers and sisters.' (Hebrews 2:11)

He knows us. He understands us. He welcomes us. He accepts us.

The Bread

When David arrives at the home of Ahimelech he asks him this question "Do you have any bread?" (v3) David is asking for bread from the priest, something to sustain him and his men.

Notice the reply of Ahimelech, "I don't have any ordinary bread." (v4) The bread that is available from the priests table is consecrated bread. It is the bread of the presence that has been placed in the Holy Place. It has been soaked in the presence of God and has therefore become special. There is something spiritual, and supernatural about this bread.

When we come to the table of our High Priest we must understand that it is not ordinary bread that He gives us. We cannot feed on ordinary things if we are going to live an extraordinary life.

He gives us 'special bread.' He gives us the bread of His Presence. He gives us something spiritual and supernatural to feed us with. He gives us Himself and says, "take and eat, this is my body." (Matthew 26:26)

The bread that He gives are His Life giving words and His life giving presence. His bread fills us and satisfies us. His bread makes us whole. His bread gives life - abundant and eternal. His bread sustains us. His bread raises us up.

There is no ordinary bread at the High Priest's table. His bread is life transforming, circumstance changing, and burden lifting.

It is interesting that the consecrated bread that David ate was meant to be only for the high priest and his family. David was actually breaking God's laws by doing what he did. And yet Jesus references this incident in the New Testament.

'Jesus answered them, "Have you never read what David did when he and his companions were hungry? He entered the house of God, and taking the consecrated bread, he ate what is lawful only for priests to eat. And he also gave some to his

companions."' (Luke 6:3-4)

Jesus doesn't criticise David for what he did. As far as Jesus is concerned, this kind of behaviour is perfectly acceptable in the presence of the High Priest. At the High Priest's table, grace is more powerful than the law, and there is enough bread for all, regardless of whether the law disqualifies us or not.

How many times do we come to church and somehow feel that we are disqualified from enjoying everything God has for us? Christians somehow feel that their sin disqualifies them from taking communion, that their lack of faith disqualifies them from receiving a miracle, or that their lack of midweek prayer and bible study disqualifies them from worshiping with joy and freedom.

All of these things may be true; it was true that the law banned David from eating that bread. But at the High Priest's table there is a higher law at work: the law of grace. It is the truth that in Christ Jesus everything that would disqualify us has been removed and nailed to the cross with Him. (Colossians 2:14) The only restrictions are the man made ones that we place on ourselves. In Christ, there is nothing to stop us enjoying everything God has for us. We are all priests in Christ's Kingdom, and at His Table even those on the run get to enjoy the Bread of His Presence.

The Sword

After David has eaten the bread, he asks another favour of the priest. He asks for a weapon. (v8)

Note the response of Ahimelech:

'The priest replied, "The sword of Goliath the Philistine, whom you killed in the Valley of Elah, is here; it is wrapped in a cloth behind the ephod. If you want it, take it; there is no sword here but that one."

David said, "There is none like it; give it to me."' (v9)

At the High Priest's table, not only does He give us bread to sustain us, but He also gives a sword to empower us. Remember that there is a special anointing at the Lord's Table. (Psalm 23) The Table can be for us a place of equipping and empowerment - a place to receive the power of the Spirit. It becomes our armour room - the place where the High Priest places something in our hands which we can use to defeat the enemy.

The sword speaks to us of the Word of God which is 'Alive and active. Sharper than any double-edged sword.' (Hebrews 4:12)

It is at the Table, as we commune and converse with our High Priest, that He speaks His words into our spirit. His words have the power to change us and transform us. His words give us strength. His words sustain us. His words empower us. His words give us courage and boldness. His words give us a weapon that we can use to fight the enemy with.

The fact that David was given Goliath's sword was very significant for him. In a time of great trial, David was reminded of one of his greatest victories. Goliath's sword became for him a word of testimony that would enable him to continue to press on into his destiny.

Every time we come to the Lord's Table and receive the bread and wine we are proclaiming the Lord's death and victory that He won at Calvary. The Bread and Wine are our testimony of what Jesus has done. Every time we eat the bread and drink the wine we are testifying that sin has been forgiven, the enemy has been defeated, and death has been robbed of its power. Therefore the Bread and Wine become a sword that we use to fight the enemy, and we overcome by the blood of the Lamb and the word of our testimony. (Revelation 12:11)

The Ephod

Finally, it is important for us to note exactly where David would find the sword 'wrapped in a cloth behind the ephod.' (v9)

The ephod was the breastplate that was worn by the High Priest. It was what covered his heart. That was where the sword was, behind the ephod.

There is a powerful principle here. If you want to get the sword that the High Priest owns, firstly you have to touch His heart.

Many today want the sword - they want the power, want a ministry, want a miracle. But where are those who will go behind the ephod? Where are those who will touch the heart of the High Priest?

In the Kingdom, power is always defined by proximity. The closer we can get to His heart, the more the power of His Spirit we can access.

This is what communion is all about. It was at the Communion Table that John the Beloved leaned in and rested his head on the beating heart of Jesus. He got behind the ephod and literally touched the heart of the High Priest.

Have you ever wondered why Peter asked John who Jesus was referring to when He told them that someone was going to betray Him? Why couldn't Peter ask Jesus himself? Proximity. We don't know where Peter was positioned at the table, but we do know where John was positioned - right next to Jesus. So close that he could lean back and touch His heart. He was so close he could receive words from Jesus that none of the others could receive because they weren't close enough.

Jesus wants to speak to us. He wants to speak words that are so intimate and powerful that they literally become like a sword in our hands. But not everyone is close enough to Him to receive those words. Only those who know the secret of communion. Only those who know what it is to get so close to Him in communion that they can lean back and feel His heartbeat. They are the ones that know what it is to get behind the ephod and touch the heart of the High Priest. In doing so, they find that they never leave His presence empty handed. They leave with the sword of the Lord - the very words of God Himself. (Ephesians 6:17) Today He invites us to lean in, lean back, to touch His heart, to listen, and to receive.

A Prayer of Response

"Jesus you are my Joseph - the source of my salvation. This world cannot satisfy me. This world is empty compared to Your Presence. But Lord, there is always bread at Your Table. I come and feast on You. You are the One who satisfies me. The free gift of the bread of life is what restores me and releases me. Thank you that You drunk the cup of wrath so that I can receive Your cup of blessing.
Jesus, my High Priest, I receive Your supernatural power and strength. I come to You and choose to lean into You. Let me feel Your heart beat and receive your words. Speak Lord, I am listening. Empower me with Your words of truth and Your words of life. Amen."

"How many are they that say: "How I should have wished to see His fair form, His figure, His clothes, His shoes!" Why here you see Him! You eat Him! And while you are longing to see His clothes He gives you Himself, not only to look at, but to touch, and to eat, and to receive within you."

- St. John of Chrysostom

12

KOINONIA

"They broke bread in their homes and ate together with glad and sincere hearts."
(Acts 2:46)

In many Communion services that I have been a part of the minister will begin the time around the Lord's Table by saying something like, 'Let us close our eyes and bow our heads. This is a personal time between you and the Lord. A time to focus, a time to examine, a time to get right with God.'

As the music plays and the bread and wine are distributed, each person is focused purely on themselves and God, hardly noticing or giving thought to the people sat around them.

But is this right? Is this Biblical? Is this how Jesus broke bread? Is this how the early Church did it?

For many the Lord's Table is something personal between us and God. We take it as individual's and are very much aware that we are remembering that Christ died for us, that Christ has saved us.

However for Jesus and the early Church, the Breaking of Bread was never just a personal thing, it was something communal. It was something to be enjoyed with and shared with others.

Even when Jesus first broke bread and distributed the cup He said, "This is my blood of the covenant, which is poured out for many." (Matthew 26:28)

Right at the introduction of what has become the Breaking of the Bread, Jesus reminds His disciples 'this is not just about you, it is about the many,' 'that is not just about each individuals personal relationship with me, I am encouraging you to look outward not just inward.'

Koinonia

Our English word "communion" is the Greek word koinonia. Used 17 times in the New Testament it was a fairly common Greek word used to describe anything from corporations to the most intimate of marriage relationships.

Koinonia is translated in more modern versions of the Bible as "fellowship," and both communion and fellowship are good translations of this word which also means to contribute, share in, and to partner with. It speaks of relationship and unity.

The New Testament uses the word koinonia not only to speak of our unity and fellowship with Christ but also our unity and fellowship with other believers.

Likewise when we gather around the Lord's Table, we are not only fellowshipping with the risen Christ, but we are fellowshipping with His Church - with each other.

These different translations reflect the nature of koinonia: it depicts an interactive relationship between God and believers who are sharing new life through Christ.

Koinonia involves active participation in Christian community, sharing in spiritual blessings, and giving material blessings.

When we gather around the Lord's Table, we are acknowledging our need of each other. We are uniting together with the Body of Christ, His Church. We are serving each other, fellowshipping with each other and receiving from each other mutual friendship.

The modern Church has in large part forgotten that there is meant to be community within the Communion.

Communion was never meant to be taken in isolation but as part of Christian community. Likewise it was never meant to be just a personal thing between us and God, but it was meant to be at the very centre of our gathering together with our brothers and sisters in Christ. This is what unites us. This is at the very heart of our meeting together.

For the early Church the Breaking of Bread was done in the context of a meal known as the Love Feast. We can see this clearly in Acts 2:

'Every day they continued to meet together in the temple courts. They broke bread in their homes and ate together with glad and sincere hearts, praising God and enjoying the favour of all the people.' (Acts 2:46-47)

Although they continued to meet in the temple, they also broke bread in people's homes. There is a deliberate contrast here between the temple, with its ceremony and its rituals and traditions and the informality of people's homes. The Breaking of Bread was not part of the traditional temple ceremony, it was relaxed, informal, enjoyable, un-traditional, and spontaneous. It spoke less of formality and more of family.

I wonder if we have transported the Breaking of Bread back into the formality of the temple instead of keeping family, relationship, and fun at the heart of the feast.

Nearly all Biblical scholars would agree that New Testament worship centred around a meal. There would be preaching, there would be singing, there would be the exercise of spiritual gifts - but the meal was right at the heart of it. The more formal moment of the breaking of bread and the drinking of wine in remembrance was done in the context of this meal, where people ate and drank together.

It is said that the family that eats together, stays together. Sadly in society now, the sitting around the table and eating together as a family is no longer common. Tragically this has also found its way into the Church. People now come to church to get their needs met and to meet with God individually. But the Lord's Table is meant to end that. Here is where we gather together as family and we rejoice together, and we weep together, and we pray together, and we learn from each other, and we carry each other, and we support each other.

In Michael Welker's book What Happens in Holy Communion? he says that the Lord's Supper is 'A communal meal, a meal that grounds community,' whilst in Todd Billings book Remembrance, Communion and Hope he says 'The Supper is a sign and action of oneness with Christ and oneness in Christ's body, the Church,' and 'For Paul, communion with the Christ leads believers to seek fellowship with other flesh and blood persons who have been adopted into God's household.' Again Billings says 'To be in communion with the beautiful, alluring Christ is impossible without communion with His broken and sinful - yet cleansed and redeemed - Bride, the Church.'

The success of the ministry of the early Church was based upon the truth that every believer saw: life is about more than self. They chose to live for something and be part of something that was much bigger than they were. When we take our eyes off of ourselves and see what God is doing through His Church and through community, we position ourselves to receive all that God has for us as individuals.

As we come to the Communion Table we are recognising our need for fellowship. Many people see Christianity as something that is intimate and personal. They see it as purely being about their relationship with God. There is a huge emphasis on the receiving of Jesus as your 'personal Saviour' and how God wants you as an individual to be blessed and prosper etc… While all of this is true, it is only one side of truth. To ignore the corporate side of faith, the coming together to fellowship with other believers, is to miss out on, not only on huge chunks of Scripture, but also on a huge part of why we were created. There can be no Christianity without community.

Adam was created in God's image. He was sinless, lived in a perfect environment, had an intimate relationship with God, and had authority and dominion. And yet despite all of that, God still said, "It is not good for the man to be alone." (Genesis 2:18)

Adam needed fellowship with another human being. Indeed Adam could not fulfil the divine mandate to 'Be fruitful and increase in number,' (Genesis 1:28) without that human fellowship. It is the same with us. It doesn't matter how close we are to God, it is not good for us to be without Christian fellowship. If God says it is not good, it is not good! We cannot fulfil our divine destiny without it.

Although worship is an intensely personal experience, it is a corporate experience also. Whenever worship is mentioned in the book of Revelation, it is in the context of believers gathering together around the throne singing songs of praise to God. Those who dislike fellowship now had better skip Heaven! In that place there will be 'A great multitude that no one could count, from every nation, tribe, people and language.' (Revelation 7:9)

The Word has to become flesh in our lives - John 1. There has to be a literal meeting together, a physical touching of the Body of Christ, relationships with real flesh and blood - pastors, brothers, and sisters.

An Unworthy Manner

For any church that takes communion on a regular basis, 1 Corinthians 11 is a familiar passage. I remember well as a child, my pastor quoting the words of Paul each week before the bread and wine were distributed:

'For I received from the Lord what I also passed on to you: The Lord Jesus, on the night He was betrayed, took bread, and when He had given thanks, He broke it and said, "This is my body, which is for you; do this in remembrance of me." In the same way, after supper He took the cup, saying, "This cup is the new covenant in my blood; do this, whenever you drink it, in remembrance of Me." For whenever you eat this bread and drink this cup, you proclaim the Lord's death until He comes.'

This was often followed by one of the most controversial and - I believe - misunderstood parts of Scripture:

'So then, whoever eats the bread or drinks the cup of the Lord in an unworthy manner will be guilty of sinning against the body and blood of the Lord. Everyone ought to examine themselves before they eat of the bread and drink from the cup.'
(V27-28)

When this part of the passage was read out, you could almost feel the tension in the air, as we were warned to 'examine ourselves' before we took Communion. What were we examining ourselves for? Well, obviously to see if we had any sin in our lives. We were warned to let the cup pass us by if we had, as taking Communion with sin in our life would result in severe punishment, for 'that is why many among you are weak and sick, and a number of you have fallen asleep.' (v30)

On occasion as a boy, I would have a cheeky look around during Communion and would observe one or two people refuse to take the bread and wine. My curiosity was pricked, 'Ah, they have obviously sinned this week! I wonder what they have done!' As I got older and began to fear the Lord, there were occasions when I would refuse Communion due to some sin that I had committed that week and the fear that I would 'sin against the body and blood of the Lord.'

As I have matured though, I have come to realise what a bizarre misunderstanding of Scripture the traditional interpretation of 1 Corinthians 11 is. Firstly, nowhere does it tell us that we are examining ourselves to see if there is any sin in our lives.

Secondly, if we have committed sin that week, the whole point of taking Communion is to remember the blood of Jesus that washes away our sin. Surely if we are convicted of sin, the answer is not to not take Communion, but to take it! If we have sinned we need Communion more than ever! We need to confess our sin, repent of it, and receive the bread and wine that testify of Jesus' sacrifice on the cross that enables our sins to be forgiven!

So if this passage is little to do with personal sin, then what is about? I believe the answer is fairly obvious. Paul says, 'For those who eat and drink without discerning the body of Christ eat and drink judgment on themselves. (v29) Other Bible translations talk about "recognising" or "appreciating" the Body of Christ. The Body of Christ, as Paul repeatedly tells us elsewhere is the Church. A closer examination of the way the Corinthians took Communion shows us what the problem was.

'So then, when you come together, it is not the Lord's Supper you eat, for when you are eating, some of you go ahead with your own private suppers. As a result, one person remains hungry and another gets drunk.' (V20-21)

When the Corinthians took Communion (which was part of an actual meal, remember) they did so in a selfish, greedy way. They came together to get their personal needs met, they came to feed themselves. There was no concern that others were not being fed; no patience in allowing others to go first, no recognition that actually this is not about me, but about the Body. This was a private thing between them and the Lord, and no acknowledgement of their brothers or sisters in the Body of Christ took place. In fact, Paul says that although they took Communion they 'despised the church of God.' (v22)

Paul had already written to them in the previous chapter about what Communion is really all about, which is much more than a personal act of devotion to God and act of remembering Jesus. The fact that there is one cup (10v16) and one loaf (v17) is a reminder that there is one Body. Taking Communion, eating of the bread, which represents His body, means that we are now partaking of the Body of Christ. It is a recognition that I am not an individual, I am joining together with the Body of which I am a part.

Now we see what Communion really is, we can see that the Corinthians' were making a mockery of Communion by giving no thought to the rest of the Body, which was the very thing that they were there to celebrate. 'Examining ourselves' therefore is not to do with unconfessed sin, but to do with examining ourselves to make sure that we are recognising, honouring, and appreciating the Body of Christ, and the love and unity that we share together. It's not about making sure I am being fed, but about contributing to meeting the needs of others.

Now we can see what 'sinning against the body and blood' is all about. Don't let Communion bypass you if you've told a lie that week; repent and get on with it! But do let Communion bypass you if you are not in right relationship with the Body of Christ. Don't take Communion if you don't honour and submit to your pastor, if you don't love your brother and sister, if you haven't forgiven that other Christian that hurt you, if you don't love and appreciate your local church, and aren't serving and contributing to the life and well-being of the Body. Otherwise, Paul's warning is very real 'That is why many among you are weak and sick, and a number of you have fallen asleep.' This may be a controversial view but I have seen it happen time and again. A failure to discern and appreciate the Body of Christ has led to Christians going through some horrendous situations that were never part of God's plan for their lives. Please don't misunderstand me. I am not saying that God necessarily punishes people who take Communion in a self-centred, individualistic way, but we must understand that the Body of Christ is our greatest protection. Satan cannot again touch the Body of Jesus Christ, and we are safe from all his attacks as we participate in His Body - through the act of Communion. But to take Communion and have no appreciation for the Body of Christ is to throw away our protection, and leave ourselves potential victims to sickness, spiritual weakness, and even premature death.

Jesus put it like this in Matthew 5:23-24, "Therefore, if you are offering your gift at the altar and there remember that your brother or sister has something against you, leave your gift there in front of the altar. First go and be reconciled to them; then come and offer your gift." The same principle can be used before we come to the Table.

J. Todd Billings also agrees that Paul's rebuke as to how the Corinthians behaved at the Table was, 'Not so much introspection about one's own unworthiness as it is for outward examination of the social dimension of covenantal fellowship…specifically do not celebrate the Supper in a way that treats brothers and sisters in Christ with indifference, failing to recognise that are also united to Christ and to oneself in covenantal fellowship. Do not celebrate in a self-serving way that neglects the poor and divides the people the Lord has united into factions.' In the words of Richard Hays, in his book First Corinthians, discerning the body means, 'recognising the community of believers for what it really is: the one Body of Christ.'

A Worthy Manner

We are given an insight into the early Church community in Acts 4:32-37;

'All the believers were one in heart and mind. No one claimed that any of their possessions was their own, but they shared everything they had. With great power the apostles continued to testify to the resurrection of the Lord Jesus. And God's grace was so powerfully at work in them all that there was no needy person among them. For from time to time those who owned land or houses sold them, brought the money from the sales and put it at the apostles' feet, and it was distributed to anyone who had need.

Joseph, a Levite from Cyprus, whom the apostles called Barnabas (which means 'son of encouragement'), sold a field he owned and brought the money and put it at the apostles' feet.'

Here we see several things about this community:

1. It was a united community - 'all the believers were one in heart and mind.'
2. It was a generous community - 'they shared everything they had.'
3. It was a grace filled community - 'God's grace was so powerfully at work.'
4. It was a Spirit filled community - 'with great power.'

5. It was a purposeful community - 'continued to testify to the resurrection.'
6. It was a healing community - 'there was no needy person.'
7. It was a giving community - 'brought the money from the sales…distributed to anyone who had need.'
8. It was a submitted community - 'put it at the apostles feet.'

Communion was a meal for the early Church, but it was more than just a meal - it was a lifestyle, with the meal at the heart of it.

The Love Feast was also known as the Agape Feast. Agape being one of the Greek words for "love" - in particular the love that cherishes, honours, respects, prizes, accepts, and is devoted to. It is the word used for Christ's love but it also the love that we should have for each other at the Table. At the Table I cherish you, I honour you, I respect you, I accept you. At the Table I reaffirm my devotion and commitment to those who I am in fellowship with as the Body of Christ.

At the Lord's Table I am showing the world a better way. I am showing honour, forgiveness, humility, submission, and meekness. At the Lord's Table I am not meant to be so focused on the bread and wine that I ignore my brother and sister, rather I am meant to share the bread and pass the cup. We are doing this together. We love one another. We are united to each other. We are devoted to each other.

'Because there is one loaf, we, who are many, are one body, for we all share the one loaf.' (1 Corinthians 10:17)

There is one loaf. At the Lord's Table, we all eat from the same loaf of bread and we are all drink from the same cup of wine. The Lord's Table is the great leveller. There is no spiritual hierarchy. We are not divided by age, gender, race, or social status. There are no denominations at the Table. There are no tribes. Theological differences are not discussed at the Table. Styles of worship are irrelevant. The one loaf testifies that we are just that - one in Christ Jesus.

The Table is where all offences should be dealt with.

> *'The Lord Jesus, on the night He was betrayed, took bread, and when He had given thanks, He broke it and said, 'This is my body, which is for you; do this in remembrance of me.' (1 Corinthians 11:23-24)*

'On the night He was betrayed.' Paul reminds us that Jesus Himself knew what it was to be betrayed and hurt by those closest to Him. But the way Jesus dealt with betrayal was the Communion Table. Jesus could not go to the cross carrying any offence, bitterness or unforgiveness in His heart towards Judas. He made sure that He sat with Judas at the Table, and offered His betrayer bread and wine.

We would do well to follow the example of Jesus and not separate ourselves from fellowship when we have been hurt or betrayed by our brothers and sisters in Christ. Instead we continue to gather around the Table, and show forgiveness and mercy to those who have wounded us so deeply. In reminding ourselves of His grace to us, we find strength to show grace to others.

For it is at the Table that Cain and Abel - the harvest and the lamb, the grain and the grape, are brought together, and the enmity between the two forever healed.

We are now one loaf - one new man, one body, foreshadowing the day when we gather together around the throne and worship the One who unites us all.

A Prayer of Response

"Jesus, thank You that I am part of Your body, the Church. Thank You that You love Your Church and died for Your Church. Give me the same heart for Your Church that You have. Let the love that You have poured into me, flow out to others. I choose to forgive those that sin against me, and ask You to heal my heart of any offence or bitterness that I may carry towards others. Holy Spirit, as I sit here at the Table, give me Your heart of love and compassion towards my brothers and sisters. Let me truly know what it is to be one in You."

"My sweetest joy is to be in the presence of Jesus in the Holy Sacrament."

- Katherine Drexel

13

THE TABLE
THE PLACE OF EXSTACTIC JOY

"And He is the head of the body, the Church."

(Colossians 1v18)

Why is it that Communion is the most somber part of many of our church services? I cannot speak for every church of course, but certainly in the ones that I have visited there is almost a depressive atmosphere that seems to creep in as soon as we approach the Lord's Table.

I have been in church services where the praise and worship was joyful and celebratory, however the moment the service switched to the Breaking of Bread, so did the tone of the music and the response of the people. Now there came a serious, reflective, almost sad atmosphere into the gathering.

I remember one time leading a Communion service and requesting that the musicians not play a quiet, reflective song about the crucifixion, but instead sing a joyful song of praise about the resurrection. Imagine my surprise when the musicians began to sing the requested song but as a quiet, slowed down ballad! When I later questioned this musical decision I was told, "It's Communion - we have to be serious!"

And Communion is a serious business. We are remembering the death of Jesus. We are looking back at the suffering and crucifixion of our Saviour and friend. It is undoubtedly a time for reflection, repentance and solemn remembrance.

But is there also a place for joy around the Lord's Table? I think that there is! After all, Jesus Himself approached the cross with joy. (Hebrews 12:2) It is also significant to remember that Christians traditionally break bread, not on the day of Jesus' crucifixion, but on Sunday, the day of His resurrection. He is alive! And He is with us! This is a reason to be joyful and to celebrate!

A Theology of Joy

Although religion often portrays Jesus as serious and somber, the book of Hebrews tells us that Jesus was anointed with joy above His companions. This means that Jesus was the most joyful person that ever walked the surface of the planet! No one will ever be as joyful as Jesus was!

This description of Jesus lines up with Luke's words in Chapter 10 of his gospel, where he writes that Jesus was 'full of joy through the Holy Spirit.' (v21) If you study the original meaning of this phrase, it seems like Jesus was filled with such an ecstatic joy that he began to leap, skip, and dance! He rejoiced with exuberance! This is the Biblical Jesus!

Jesus' heart for His disciples is that we would experience this same joy. In John 15 He says, "I have told you this so that my joy may be in you and that your joy may be complete." (v11)

The desire of Jesus was that the same ecstatic, exuberant joy that caused Him to leap and skip and dance would be in every one of us! His longing was that we would experience this joy and that our joy would be complete, or as the Amplified puts it 'complete, full, and overflowing.'

God's desire that all of His children experience true joy is throughout the pages of Scripture. Nehemiah famously tells us that it is the joy of the Lord that gives us strength, (Nehemiah 8:10) while Proverbs 17:22 tells us that 'A cheerful heart is good medicine.'

Jesus, Joy, and Communion

How then does this reflect our attitude as we come around the Lord's Table? Should it be a time of great celebration as well as a time of more somber reflection? I certainly believe so!

Let us begin by looking for a moment at the Gospels and the way Jesus ate dinner with His companions. Remember that for the New Testament Church, the Lord's Table was part of an actual meal, a Love Feast. Eating and drinking was at the centre of the life and ministry of Jesus.

Jesus was so famous for His dinner parties that He even had a reputation as a party animal! It was said of Jesus, 'Here is a glutton and a drunkard.' (Luke 7:34) Now I am certain that Jesus was neither of these things, but He must have done something for people to speak of Him like that. It seems his dinner parties were pretty raucous occasions! Would a man, who just nibbled on a piece of bread and sipped at his drink really be accused of being a glutton and a drunk?! No of course not! When Jesus ate with His friends, there was plenty of food and drink, there was laughter, there was joy and there was celebration. It was not a dead, stuffy, religious gathering, but a party full of life and freedom!

In one of Jesus' most famous parables, the story of the Prodigal Son, He describes the response of the Father after his wayward son has finally returned home. Jesus tells us that there was a feast! A celebration! The household was filled with gladness at the returning son. There was plenty of food to eat, as the fattened calf was killed and meanwhile the whole house was filled with the sound of music and dancing. This was a party full of laughter and joy!

In the context of this parable in Luke 15, Jesus it seems is telling us that this is what Heaven is like! Whenever a sinner repents on earth, Heaven is filled with celebration and rejoicing. The sound of Heaven is the sound of joy!

In another parable, Jesus described His Kingdom as a wedding banquet. (Matthew 22) Have you ever been to a wedding banquet? There are certainly moments of seriousness, reflection, and tenderness. But the whole thing is undergirded by joy! It is a day to celebrate and be happy. And at some point during the festivities all sense of propriety is thrown to one side as the Bride, Bridegroom, and guests throw themselves fully into the joy of the occasion.

Fast forward two thousand years to a modern day Communion service. A slow, reflective piece of music is played in the background. The congregation is sat with their eyes closed and heads bowed. A tiny piece of bread is given to each person whilst they are invited to take a tiny sip of watered down grape juice. The whole occasion is serious, solemn, and sober.

Now take the Jesus of the Bible. The Jesus who was described as the most joyful person who ever lived. The Jesus who danced and skipped with an ecstatic joy. The Jesus who's meal times were so wild that He was accused of being a glutton and a drunk. The Jesus who told stories of feasts and parties and celebrations. Take this Jesus and transport Him to one of our Communion services. Do you think He would fit in? Do you think He would recognise it? Do you think He would enjoy it? "We are doing this in your honour Jesus!" "We are remembering you." "We've put your Name on this!"

Is this what He had in mind when He instituted the Breaking of Bread? If we can't see the Biblical Jesus in our Church culture, then the Church culture has to change.

I am 100% convinced that if Jesus were to step into one of our pulpits and host a Communion service, there would be a huge element of joy and celebration in the midst of the seriousness and reflection.

Joy in Communion

As we leave behind the gospels and move further into the New Testament we also get glimpses of how the early Church approached the Lord's Table.

There is a wonderful glimpse of how the first disciples took Communion in Acts 2:46; they broke bread in their homes and ate together with glad and sincere hearts. The Greek word for "glad" is the word agalliasis, and it is the same word translated as "joy" that is used of Jesus in Luke 10:21. It is describing a very expressive, demonstrative, and highly celebratory joy. Often this word is linked with dancing.

This is how the early Church broke bread! Is there a place in our Breaking of Bread services for dancing as we come around the Table? Is there a place for people to celebrate and exercise great joy?

As we move into the Epistles, Paul's first letter to the Corinthians contains a stinging rebuke over how they acted at the Lord's Table. In Chapter 11, Paul describes the sorry state of this church's Communion services. He says that some people ate so much food that there was none left for anyone else. He then describes how some drank so much wine that they became drunk. Paul uses the strongest possible terms to rebuke them for their excess.

Whilst the Corinthians were undoubtedly wrong in their approach to the Communion Table it does make you think as to what the early Church believed Communion was all about. If Communion was seen as a time to be serious and sober, it seems strange that the Corinthian church had become so excessive in their behaviour. Is it not more likely that for all the churches in the New Testament, the Lord's Table was seen as a place of joy, feasting and celebration but in their enthusiasm the Corinthians had gone overboard, and allowed carnality to creep in? The solution, surely, is not to deny the flesh at the expense of joy, but to allow the joy, celebration, feasting, eating, drinking, and laughter to remain, but to make sure that it is all done in a 'beautiful and orderly way.' (1 Corinthians 14:40 - TPT)

Remember With Joy

One of the most important aspects of the Communion Table is that it is where we look back to the cross of Calvary and remember the death of Jesus. Although this should produce within us strong feelings of emotion and brokenness at what Jesus went through, it should also produce within us joy and gladness. After all the Cross was not a tragedy but a victory! Through His death we have forgiveness of sins, eternal life, and reconciliation with God as our Father. Our Saviour is not dead, He is alive, He has conquered sin, He has conquered death, and He has defeated the devil!

Can you remember when you first gave your life to Jesus? Can you remember the joy that you experienced?

One of my favourite stories is found in the writings of the great Richard Wurmbrand who spent many years in prison for his faith in Communist Romania. In the book Jesus Freaks, compiled by the singing group DC Talk, Wurmbrand tells the following story:

'When I was still living behind the Iron Curtain, I had met a Russian captain. He loved God, he longed after God, but he had never seen a Bible. He had never attended religious services. He had no religious education, but he loved God without the slightest knowledge of Him.

I read to him the Sermon on the Mount and the parables of Jesus. After hearing them, he danced around the room in rapturous joy, proclaiming, 'What a wonderful beauty! How could I live without knowing this Christ?' It was the first time that I saw someone jubilating in Christ.

Then I made a mistake. I read to him the passion and crucifixion of Christ, without having prepared him for this. He had not expected it. When he heard how Christ was beaten, how He was crucified, and that in the end He died, he fell in an armchair and began to weep bitterly. He had believed in a Saviour and now his Saviour was dead!

I looked at him and was ashamed that I called myself a Christian and a pastor, a teacher of others. I had never shared the sufferings of Christ as this Russian officer now shared them. Looking at him was, for me, like seeing Mary Magdalene weeping at the foot of the cross or at the empty tomb.

Then I read to him the story of the resurrection. When he heard this wonderful news, that the Saviour arose from the tomb, he slapped his knees, and shouted for joy: "He is alive! He is alive!" Again he danced around the room, overwhelmed with happiness!

I said to him, "Let us pray!"

He fell on his knees together with me. He did not know our holy phrases. His words of prayer were, "O God, what a fine chap You are! If I were You and You were me, I would never have forgiven You Your sins. But You are really a very nice chap! I love You with all my heart."

I think that all the angels in heaven stopped what they were doing to listen to this sublime prayer from the Russian officer. When this man received Christ, he knew he would immediately lose his position as an officer, that prison and perhaps death in jail would almost surely follow. He gladly paid the price. He was ready to lose everything.'

I have shared this story many times in my sermons. It is always a challenging reminder for those of us who have heard the gospel message so many times that it may have become over familiar. When that happens we can lose the sense of joy that comes from knowing Jesus.

Joy and salvation are often linked together in the scriptures. David famously prayed that God would restore unto him the joy of his salvation. (Psalm 51:12) Like the Russian officer, are we still filled with such an overwhelming sense of joy and happiness when we think of Jesus? Do we want to dance, and sing, and shout because of how happy we are because of what Jesus has done?

Or has the gospel become so familiar to us that we have lost that childlike giddiness and sense of exuberance in the presence of God?

I believe that the Lord's Table contains a deep well that we can come and drink from.

'With joy you draw water from the well of salvation.' (Isaiah 12:3)

At the Lord's Table as we reflect on what Jesus did for us on the Cross, we are doing more than just mentally remembering a historical event. Our spirit man is being lowered into the well of God's redeeming love and we are drinking from the source of salvation and grace. As we do so, a restoration is taking place deep within us, and as we continue to drink, joy will bubble up on the outside as God fills and re-fills us with the joy of our salvation. A joy that is in Him, 'Joy inexpressible and full of glory.' (1 Peter 1:8 - NKJV) Or as the Passion Translation puts it, 'You are saturated with an ecstatic joy, indescribably sublime and immersed in glory.'

Commune With Joy

The Lord's Table is not just a time for remembering and looking back, but of present fellowship with the Risen Saviour. As we have said elsewhere in this book there is a communion within the Communion. The Lord's Table is a time when we can quiet our spirits, wait on the presence of Jesus and have Him speak to us as we fellowship with His Holy Spirit. John the Baptist described his experience of communing with Jesus like this:

'The friend who attends the bridegroom waits and listens for him, and is full of joy when he hears the bridegroom's voice. That joy is mine, and it is now complete.'
(John 3:29)

The stress and busyness of our normal week can so easily rob us of our joy, but when we have communion with the Lord His voice speaks into our spirit, and at the sound of His voice our hearts are filled with overwhelming and overflowing joy.

In Psalm 36:8, David describes the house of God as a banqueting hall, a place where a feast is provided for God's children. It is as we eat at this table that we drink from a river of delights, or as another translation puts it, 'They feast on the bounty of your house; you let them drink from your river of pure joy.' (CEB)

God's gift of wine was given to gladden the heart of man, (Psalm 104:15) while in Psalm 4:7 both the wine (the blood) and the grain (the bread/body) are mentioned together:

'You have filled my heart with greater joy than when their grain and new wine abound.'

The harvest seasons of grain and new wine were always associated with joy, celebration, and gratitude. How much greater the joy produced by God's greatest gifts - the bread of His Body and wine of His blood. Surely they should cause our hearts to overflow with joy and celebration.

As I mentioned at the start of this book, my purpose in writing is not to tell any believer or church how they should take Communion. My purpose is to cause us to think: Is there something that we are missing when we break bread? Are there some things that we need to re-discover?

I believe that joy around the Communion Table is undoubtedly something that we need a revival of. As I read Scripture I always see the Bread and Wine associated with joy. I read of a joyful Saviour who invited people to a Kingdom centred around a joyful wedding banquet. I see an early Church that broke bread with joy. I see a call to remember the joy of our salvation and an invitation to fellowship with the One in whose presence there is fullness of joy.

Perhaps in the reverence and solemnity of the Lord's Table, we can also rediscover this sense of joy and celebration. Perhaps amidst the reflection, we can also find time for singing and dancing.

'Because they were wondering and questioning in the midst of their happiness, He said to them, "Do you have anything to eat?' (Luke 24:41 – CEB)

A Prayer of Response

"Holy Spirit, restore unto me the joy of salvation. Let me never forget what Jesus did for me. Let me never forget all that is available in Him. Let me never lose that sense of joy at the thought of my Saviour. Holy Spirit, in Your presence is fullness of joy. Fill me with that joy as I commune with You. Let me hear Your voice, for in hearing You, true joy is found. Your joy is my strength and my healing. I feast on You and receive your joy. Amen."

"Christ held Himself in His hands when He gave His Body to His disciples saying: "this is My Body." No one partakes of this Flesh before he has first adored it."

- *St. Augustine*

14

THE TABLE
A PLACE OF EXTRAVAGANT WORSHIP

*'Enter His gates with thanksgiving and His courts with praise;
give thanks to Him and praise His name.'*

(Psalm 100:4)

Psalm 100 gives us the path that God made to enable us to enter into His presence. It all begins with thanksgiving. Thanksgiving for all that God has done will lead to praise for all that He is. This will enable us to enter into His presence where we can enjoy sweet communion with Him.

If we can use Psalm 100 as our template for worship and communion then we can see that it all starts with thanksgiving. Thanksgiving is the starting point of communion. We will only go as deep into the presence of God as much as we have first given thanks. Thanksgiving is the gate - the access point of communion. We can only enter into the communion experience and access all the wonderful blessings and bliss of spending time with Him once we have first given thanks.

The word Eucharist has been used by some denominations to refer to the act of the giving and receiving of the sacraments themselves, but Eucharist comes from the Greek noun which means thanksgiving. Eucharist is not meant to be the act of eating and drinking, but rather the attitude in which we eat and drink. We are meant to approach the Communion Table with a heart bursting with thankfulness and praise.

Thanksgiving

In 1 Corinthians 10, the Apostle Paul refers to the cup that we drink from at the Communion Table as 'the cup of thanksgiving.' This is such a beautiful description of how we are to drink at the Lord's Supper. We drink with a heart that is overwhelmed with thankfulness for all that Jesus has done for us.

Jesus Himself knew what is was to break the bread and drink the cup with great thankfulness.

All four of the gospels share the incredible miracle of Jesus feeding the five thousand with just five loaves of bread and two small fish. The miracle stands alone as a powerful testimony of both the compassion and the power of Jesus - He not only desires to meet our lack, but He also has the ability to supernaturally provide and meet every one of our needs. However, perhaps there is also prophetic symbolism taking place as Jesus breaks the bread before distributing. Perhaps this is a foreshadowing of His own Body that would be broken, like the bread was, and given to all who would come and eat. This broken body would meet man's ultimate need of forgiveness and salvation.

It is significant for us to note that in John's account of this miracle, the evangelist records, 'Jesus then took the loaves, gave thanks, and distributed to those that were seated as much as they wanted.' (John 6:11) Before people were given the bread, Jesus gave thanks for it. This may seem like an incidental detail, but John clearly took note of this as he mentions it again later in the chapter, 'Then some boats from Tiberius landed near the place where the people had eaten the bread after the Lord had given thanks.' (John 6:23)

Twice John refers to Jesus giving thanks as He broke bread. Why would he mention this twice? Is he showing us a principle: this is how you break bread. You do so with a heart of thankfulness.

During the Last Supper itself, it says of Jesus, 'Then he took a cup, and when He had given thanks, He gave it to them, saying, "Drink from it, all of you."' (Matthew 26:27)

Now we have the cup, but again Jesus is doing the same thing - giving thanks to the Father.

He gave thanks for the bread. He gave thanks for the wine.

In all of these scriptures the Greek word Eucharisteo is used, which is where we get our word Eucharist from. It effectively means three things - to be thankful, to feel grateful, and to give thanks.

Just pause for a moment and think about that. To be. To feel. To give.

To be - we are grateful. This is who I am, my identity as I approach the Table. I am thankful, I am grateful for all that Jesus has done, all that the Father gave, all that is available through the Spirit.

To feel - this is not just a cold, religious ceremony. I feel something. My heart has been set on fire with this love and I burn with thankfulness and gratitude. Thankfulness, praise, and worship fill my entire being.

To give - this is my response. I am not just a grateful person who feels thankful, I actually give thanks. I open my mouth and give thanks to Him in prayer and song. I also give Him my heart, my affection, my very life. This is my thankful response to all that He has done.

The word Eucharisteo also contains within it another Greek word 'charis' which is translated in English 'grace.' The word charis itself also contains within it the word chara, which means 'joy.'

Putting these different translations and words together, we can sum up how God expects us to break bread and drink wine like this:

I am grateful for all that God has done for me. My heart burns and bursts with thankfulness because of the amazing grace that I have received in Jesus. Now through the joy of the Holy Spirit I open my mouth, and give Him thanks and praise, and joyfully give to Him all that I have and all that I am.

Praise

After the resurrection, Jesus appears on the Road to Emmaus and appears to two of His disciples who do not recognise Him. It was as Jesus broke bread with them that they realised who He was. But let's read that verse carefully and note something:

> 'When He was at the table with them, He took bread, gave thanks, broke it and began to give it to them.' (Luke 24:30)

Once again we see Jesus giving thanks as He broke bread. Perhaps it was a combination of the two things - the giving of thanks and the breaking of the bread together that caused the two men to realise. This is the Jesus way, this is how He does it.

The breaking of bread and the drinking of the cup was never intended to be something cold, passive, and formal. It was meant to be a time of joyful thanksgiving and overwhelming gratitude.

When Luke talks of Jesus giving thanks here, he uses a slightly different Greek word to eucharisteo. This time he uses the word eulogeo. Although this word is probably best translated 'thanks,' it is slightly different to the word eucaharisteo, as eulogeo also contains an element of praise. Indeed there is even an element of celebration as eulogeo means to give thanks as you celebrate with praise.

Remember Psalm 100, we enter His gates with thanksgiving in our hearts, and we enter His courts with praise. The Lord's Table is meant to contain both of these elements of adoration - it is where we thank God for what He has done, but also where we praise Him for all that He is. He is our Saviour. He is our Redeemer. He is our Champion.

The word eulogeo can also mean 'to bless.' This is why some translations refer to Paul's 'cup of thanksgiving' as the 'cup of blessing.' Though the blessing of eulogeo is very much linked with our words - we speak a blessing or we speak favour over something or someone.

I have been to many communion services which were conducted in silence as partakers were encouraged to bow their heads and silently reflect on the Cross. Although the Lord's Table is a time to reflect, it was not meant to be a time to be silent - it was meant to be a time when we opened our mouths and gave praise to God, thanking Him for who He is and declaring His blessing and favour over our lives.

Paul himself tells us that the Lord's Supper should be accompanied by proclamation: 'Whenever you eat this bread and drink this cup, you proclaim the Lord's death.' (1 Corinthians 11:26) You proclaim: announce, declare, make known publicly.

Communion was not just meant to be a private act of devotion, but a public demonstration of praise.

The highpoint of our praise should be the Lord's Table. It should be the most passionate, and powerful time of praise in our church services.

The word eulogeo can also mean 'to release divine favour.' Even the words for 'prosperity,' and 'well-being' are found in the root of this word.

Is there a link between our attitude to the Lord's Table and our finances? Is there a connection between how we take communion and physical and emotional well-being? Can taking communion in the right spirit release God's favour?

This is for each reader to study for themselves and see what the scriptures say, but it seems quite possible there is a connection here. After all it was as Jesus gave thanks, and broke bread, that supernatural provision came and there was a multiplication of their resources.

Is God showing us that as we release praise at the Lord's Table His divine favour is released over us? And would this in turn enables us to enjoy prosperity, and provision in our finances, and receive health and wholeness in our bodies and souls?

Worship

Many teachers on adoration would say that the correct protocol in approaching God is to begin with thanksgiving, and then this will lead into praise. This in turn will then lead into worship, which is the ultimate expression of love for Him.

We have already seen that our time of Communion should involve both thanksgiving and praise. But one of the most powerful descriptions of worship in the New Testament is also centered around the Table.

'When one of the Pharisees invited Jesus to have dinner with Him, He went to the Pharisee's house and reclined at the table. A woman in that town who lived a sinful life learned that Jesus was eating at the Pharisee's house, so she came there with an alabaster jar of perfume. As she stood behind Him at his feet weeping, she began to wet His feet with her tears. Then she wiped them with her hair, kissed them and poured perfume on them.' (Luke 7:36-38)

Mark's description of what Mary did in the Passion Translation is as follows, 'She walked right up to Jesus, and with a gesture of extreme devotion, and she broke the flask and poured out the precious oil over his head.' (Mark 14:3 - TPT)

Mary's worship was costly and extravagant. It was a gesture of 'extreme devotion.' She displayed such vulnerability, sacrifice, humility, and tenderness. This was an act of love and adoration.

Perhaps Mary did not realise that she was fulfilling prophecy but there is an obvious parallel with what she did and the words of Song of Songs 1:12, 'While the king was at his table, my perfume spread its fragrance.'

Now hundreds of years after Solomon penned these lyrics, Mary approaches the Great King above all kings at His Table, and pours out her perfume of worship and extreme devotion.

Jesus Himself describes Mary's act as 'lavish devotion, (Mark 14:9 - TPT) and announced that what she did would be forever remembered and preached where the gospel went. Why? Is Jesus wanting us to recognise that this is what we do at the King's Table? Here we worship. And we worship extravagantly, lavishly, and passionately. With songs, tears, and the outpouring of our devotion - we pour everything out on Jesus.

John's account of this story contains a throw away comment that I believe is so powerful, 'The fragrance of the costly oil filled the house.' (John 12:3 - TPT) As Mary adored Jesus, something changed in that room. There was a noticeable shift in the atmosphere. The room began to smell different. Something tangible had happened.

In our public gatherings the act of Communion is meant to be a game changer. As the saints gather around the Lord's Table the atmosphere in the service should change. Things should feel different, even smell different (spiritually speaking), as there has been a shift, heavenly perfume has been released. Something has filled the house that wasn't there before.

Sadly I have been in many Communion services where the opposite has happened - the atmosphere has changed but in a negative way. I have been in times of praise that have been so powerful but then it has been announced that we are going to 'Come around the Table.' Suddenly the worship has stopped, the praise has ended. People have sat down and bowed their heads silently and reverently, and become introspective as they begin to quietly ponder and internally confess their sins.

But Communion is meant to be about praise! It is meant to be about thanksgiving. It should be the highlight of every public gathering - here is where my worship gets serious! I am approaching the King at His Table and here I am going to pour out everything. Here is where He gets all of my love and all of my devotion. My most powerful, joyful, intimate, and passionate worship is meant to take place at the Table.

Those who truly get the Lord's Table may even be accused of being too excessive and over the top by those who don't understand the value God places on communion. After all, Mary's act of worship was considered a waste by others. But to Jesus it was a beautiful thing. May we all provide the Lord with beautiful moments of worship at His Table.

Surrender

The Communion Table is certainly a place for extravagant worship. But let us also remember what true worship is according to the New Testament. Although the singing of songs is no doubt an important part of our adoration to God, remember the words of Paul in Romans 12:

> *'Therefore, I urge you, brothers and sisters, in view of God's mercy, to offer your bodies as a living sacrifice, holy and pleasing to God–this is your true and proper worship.' (Romans 12:1)*

According to Paul, true worship is more than just singing songs, it is living a life of consecration in surrender to God.

Mary's act of devotion was a sacrifice, it cost her something. Now all of us are called to give our whole lives to God as living sacrifices. This is true worship and devotion.

As we come around the Communion Table, not only do we come bringing thanksgiving and praise, but we also come to surrender our lives in dedication to our King.

Paul writes strongly in 1 Corinthians:

> *'You cannot drink the cup of the Lord and the cup of demons too; you cannot have a part in both the Lord's Table and the table of demons. Are we trying to arouse the Lord's jealousy? Are we stronger than He?' (1 Corinthians 10:21-22)*

Paul is writing to a culture where the worship of idols was common place. In this section of 1 Corinthians he is making two points. On one hand, he is saying that idols are not real gods, therefore eating food or drinking drinks that have been offered to idols has no supernatural power. But in case they misunderstood him, he makes it very clear in verses 21-22, you cannot continue to worship idols and then worship Jesus at the Lord's Table.

Paul is making a clear statement to the Corinthians, you choose who you worship, Jesus or idols, but it cannot be both. And the Communion Table is the dividing line, the wall of separation. It is at the Table that I choose – I am no longer putting my trust in idols, but I am putting my trust in Jesus. Here at the Table I give myself to Him. He is my source. He is the object of my worship.

It is important to note that it is the "Lord's" Table. At the Table, He is the Friend of Sinners who welcomes all, but He is also the Lord. He is the One who demands my allegiance, my worship, and my very life.

In our culture we have our own idols. Idols of sex, money, greed, power, and entertainment. Perhaps the greatest idol of all is the idol of self. Everyday the flesh screams at us to sit down and dine with these gods; to indulge them, just a little.

But as we approach the Communion Table we have a choice. I can either go to the table of false gods, and eat, drink, and satisfy my flesh or I can turn my back on the table of this world and go instead to the Lord's Table. I can recognise that He is my source, He is my God, He is the One I trust, He is the One I obey, He is the One I serve.

Paul makes it clear that we cannot eat from both tables. We cannot drink from both cups. We cannot be like the children of Israel who on the one hand, 'Ate the same spiritual food and drank the same spiritual drink,' (1 Corinthians 10:3-4) and on the other hand, 'Sat down to eat and drink and got up to indulge in pagan revelry,' (v7) and committed sexual immorality. (v8)

Paul tells us that God was not pleased with them (v5) and their bodies were left 'scattered over the desert.' 'These things happened to them as examples and were written down as warnings for us.' (v11)

The Lord's Table is where I decide who I serve and who I belong to. It is where I choose who I worship and who I trust. It was where I either feed self or deny self.

In his book Remembrance, Communion, and Hope - J.Todd Billings says the following:

'Union with Christ – like marital love – requires exclusive allegiance, a self-offering in worship to the Lord rather than to other gods. One becomes united with demons and idols OR the body and blood of Christ and all who partake of the body and blood of Christ.

Our bodies belong to Jesus Christ, our spouse, who offers His own body as food and drink. Our bodies are thus temples of Christ's presence by the Spirit, and our lives should be given in self-offering worship to the Lord and in fellowship with His people, acting as witnesses to Christ in a sinful world. The body, as the Spirit's temple, can be contaminated with idolatry; the body can be united to Christ's body, or united with a prostitute's body in betrayal of the Christian's true spouse. Both bodily actions involve spurring the life giving self-offering of the Lord Jesus Christ, just as the Israelites spurned the spiritual food and spiritual drink offered by the covenant Lord.'

At the Lord's Table I recognise that He is my God and He is stronger than I am. (1 Corinthians 10:22) I yield to His strength and His Lordship and in the words of the Heidelberg Catechism, 'I am not my own, but belong - body and soul, in life and in death - to my faithful Saviour, Jesus Christ.'

In conclusion, my response to the broken bread and the poured out wine is to become broken bread and poured out wine: to live my life in surrender and devotion to Him.

Paul's Choice

As we close this chapter on adoration and worship we know that worship is a choice that we all have to make. Sometimes it is easy and sometimes it is difficult. It is easy to praise God when our circumstances are good and everything seems to be going fine. But what about when it seems like everything in our lives is falling apart? What about when we are going through hardship, or adversity?

The Apostle Paul is an incredible example of someone who chose to worship and praise God even in the midst of great distress. His difficulties were many and varied but there are so many wonderful scriptures about how Paul chose thanksgiving and joy no matter what he was faced with.

One of the greatest examples is found in Acts 27. In this chapter, Paul is on a ship that goes through a powerful hurricane. The Bible tells us that they took a 'violent battering.' They go on to throw their cargo overboard. All is in darkness as they see neither sun or stars for many days. They reach the point of giving up all hope of being saved. (v20)

I wonder if Paul's situation can sometimes describe our lives? Do you ever feel like you are being tossed about by the circumstances of life? Do you ever feel like you are losing everything of value? Do you ever feel like you are going through a violent battering? Do you ever feel like you are in darkness and you can't see the way out? Have you lost hope that things will ever change?

We can learn from Paul's wonderful example. Verse 35 tells us the choice Paul made, 'He took some bread and gave thanks to God in front of them all. Then he broke it and began to eat.'

In the midst of this great trial, Paul chose to break bread and give thanks to God. The Aramaic says that 'he glorified God.'

Paul chose not to focus on the storm but on His Saviour. He chose to trust His Lord and what He had promised rather than give in to fear. It is one thing to give thanks when the sun is shining, but in the midst of tribulation - to break bread and give thanks to God - this is a man who knows the power of communion, and the power of worship.

Imagine if when we next go through a storm, instead of panic and fear, we respond by coming to the Lord's Table and praising Him.

Imagine the scenario as the sound of the wind and the waves was drowned out by the sound of one man, worshipping and adoring His God. The sounds of weeping and wailing were replaced by the sound of praise.

What was the result? 'They were all encouraged and ate some food themselves.' (v37)

The atmosphere on the boat changed! There was a shift. Now hope had come. Courage had come. This is the power of Communion and worship!

Paul's declaration of praise was followed by the deliverance of everyone on board. Every person was saved as they landed on the Island of Malta, where Paul goes on to have a healing revival!

This is a mighty testimony of the saving power of God. And Paul found that power because he had found the secret of knowing what it is to break bread and worship even in the darkness.

A Prayer of Response

"Father I thank You for all that you have done. Thank You for sending Jesus to die for me. Thank Your wonderful gift of salvation. Jesus I praise You for all that you are. You are my Saviour, My Redeemer and my friend. I worship you Holy God. I love You, I adore You. Jesus you are my Lord. I surrender to You. I give my life and my all to You. I turn my back on this world and I pledge my allegiance to You King Jesus. Father, no matter what I am going through, no matter my circumstances, I choose to praise You. I choose to fellowship with You. Your grace is always enough. Amen."

"I hunger for the bread of God, the flesh of Jesus Christ. I long to drink of His blood, the gift of unending love."

- *St. Ignatius of Antioch*

15
HUNGRY AND THIRSTY FOR JESUS

"Come, all you who are thirsty, come to the waters; and you who have no money, come, buy and eat! Come, buy wine and milk without money and without cost."

(Isaiah 55:1)

As we have already covered in this book, the Lord's Table is a looking back to the death of Jesus and the covenant made in His blood. The Lord's Table is also about encountering the risen Saviour in the here and now. However, the Lord's Table is also a looking forward – ahead, to the return of the King of King's and the Lord of Lord's.

As wonderful as it us for to come to the Lord's Table we know that we are only to do this 'Until He comes,' (1 Corinthians 11:26) for 'When that which is perfect is come, then that which is in part shall be done away.' (1 Corinthians 13:10 - KJV)

For just as the Jewish Passover passed away to be replaced by the New Testament 'Breaking of bread,' so too this will pass away, to be replaced by the Wedding Banquet of the Lamb.

The Foretaste

As wonderful as our times of communion with the Lord are now, they are just a foretaste of what is to come. When the children of Israel ate Manna in the wilderness, it is no coincidence that it tasted like wafers made with honey. (Exodus 16:31) This sweet taste was a foreshadowing of the Promised Land, a land that would flow with milk and honey. (Exodus 3:8)

Likewise every time we eat the bread and drink the wine at the Communion table, we are looking ahead to that day when we shall eat and drink with Him at the Marriage Supper in Heaven, when we shall see Him face to face, and dine with Him forever. As J. Todd Billings puts it, 'The Lord's Supper, as a foretaste of the Wedding Banquet of the Lamb and His Bride, gives us a taste of God's new world.'

On that day I will sit and dine with Jesus at His Banqueting Table. This is His great promise, not only to the Twelve, but to all who a part of His Bride.

'I tell you, I will not drink from this fruit of the vine from now on until that day when I drink it new with you in my Father's kingdom.' (Matthew 26:29)

'And I confer on you a kingdom, just as my Father conferred one on me, so that you may eat and drink at My table in My kingdom and sit on thrones, judging the twelve tribes of Israel.' (Luke 22:29-30)

On that day every longing of the soul shall be met and we shall be eternally satisfied in His presence as Isaiah foretold:

'They will neither hunger nor thirst, nor will the desert heat or the sun beat down on them. He who has compassion on them will guide them and lead them beside springs of water.' (Isaiah 49:10)

Truly we shall be one with Him. As J. Todd Billings puts it, 'Communion is rooted in hope that the present sweet fellowship will culminate in spousal intimacy.'

When Israel celebrated the Passover, God instructed them to eat the lamb and the unleavened bread alongside bitter herbs. (Numbers 9:11) This was an interesting contrast - the succulent meat and the satisfying bread, but then the bitter after-taste of the herbs.

When we come to the Lord's Table we do so with joy and thanksgiving, our hearts satisfied and overwhelmed by His love. And yet as we leave the Table, there is a bitter after-taste. We still live in a world dominated by sin. We still suffer the effects of the Fall. Our bodies know what it is to get weak, sick, and feel pain. We all know the bitterness of loved ones dying, the despair of grief and the reminder of our own mortality.

'Christ is present at the Supper, but there is also a sense in which Christ is absent - and the final culmination of His Kingdom is longed for in and through the Supper.'
- J. Todd Billings

For as we taste the bitterness of this world, the Lord's Table fills us with hope. A hope that is spoken of in Isaiah 25:

'On this mountain the Lord Almighty will prepare a feast of rich food for all peoples, a banquet of aged wine – the best of meats and the finest of wines. On this mountain He will destroy the shroud that enfolds all peoples, the sheet that covers all nations; He will swallow up death for ever. The Sovereign Lord will wipe away the tears from all faces; He will remove His people's disgrace from all the earth. The Lord has spoken.' (v6-8)

Isaiah spoke of another Communion meal, the Wedding Banquet of the Lamb. There shall be no bitter herbs eaten with this meal, for on that day every tear shall be wiped away. On that day death will be defeated forever. There shall be no more pain, no more sickness, no more disease, and no more death. There shall be no more bitter partings.

On that day we will truly be able to say:

> 'Surely this is our God; we trusted in Him, and He saved us. This is the Lord, we trusted in Him; let us rejoice and be glad in His salvation.' (v9)

The Longing

In the meantime we long for Christ and His Return, and we ache to taste from that great Wedding Banquet. Our prayer, when we come around the Lord's Table is simply, 'Come, Lord Jesus.' (Revelation 22:20)

Every time we approach the Lord's Table we should do so with a ravenous appetite and a desperate thirst; hungry for a taste of Him and thirsty for His presence, longing to meet and commune with our God.

We come hungry and thirsty, trusting the promises of the Bible that those who hunger and thirst for righteousness shall be filled, (Matthew 5:6) and that He satisfies the thirsty and fills the hungry with good things. (Psalm 107:9)

In my house I have a one year old boy. When he is hungry he cries out and his mother will feed him until he is full. I also have a four year boy. When he is hungry he cries out and his mother will feed him until he is full. And then there is me! When I am hungry, I too will cry out and their mother will feed me until I am full!

Three men, all hungry, all eat until they are filled. But what satisfies a one year old will not satisfy a four year old. And what satisfies a four year old will not satisfy a grown man.

As we grow older, our capacity for food increases. In the same way as we grow in our walk with Jesus, our capacity for Him should increase more and more. We do not want to be decades old in our walk with Jesus and yet have the spiritual appetite and capacity of a baby. I should be more hungry and thirsty for Jesus now than when I first came to know Him.

One of the signs of illness can be a loss of appetite. A believer or church that has lost its hunger and thirst for Jesus is surely an unhealthy one. We need to re-visit the Lord's Table, and eat with Him. I have noticed that if I fast for a long period of time my capacity for food diminishes. But the more I eat the more my capacity grows!

Every time I come to the Lord's Table, I leave more and more satisfied, and yet at the same time continually longing for more of Him.

As Gregory of Nyssa said, 'To those who have tasted and seen by experience "that the Lord is sweet," (Psalm 34:8), this taste becomes a kind of invitation to further enjoyment. And thus the one who is rising toward God constantly experiences this continual incitement toward further progress.'

J. Todd Billings writes, 'We feed upon Christ, who brings life, and whose life in us by the Spirit bears fruit in acts of witness and love in the world; and yet, this feeding ultimately makes us more and more hungry.'

And, 'In hope, God's people enjoy a foretaste of heavenly manna, a taste that deepens our hunger and focuses our desires on the Kingdom that only Jesus Christ can bring.'

Gloriously Full - Ravenously Hungry

There was once a man who had worked all his life for the same company. Upon his retirement the company decided to thank him for his years of hard service by giving him a free ticket for a round the world cruise.

On the first evening on board the luxury ship, the man went into the restaurant and sat down to eat. As he looked at the menu however his heart sank. He could not afford any of the delicious items on the menu. The only thing he could afford was the soup and a bread roll. So that is what he ordered.

Night after night as the ship made its voyage around the world, the man would sit in the restaurant and order soup and a bread roll.

On the last night of the cruise as the man sat at the table, he decided he would be a little bit bold. After all, it was the last night, he had nothing to lose. When the waiter came to take his order the man spoke up, "Sir, I was wondering something. I would love one of the wonderful steaks I see coming out of the kitchen but I just can't afford one. At the end of service tonight, when the restaurant closes, if there is any steak left over, could I have it for free?'

The waiter paused for a moment. He had become fond of the old guy, and the food would only go to waste. "I don't see why not," he replied, "just one thing. I need to see that you have a valid ticket. If I was caught giving food to a stowaway I'd lose my job."

The man handed him his ticket and the waiter looked at it for some moments with a look of confusion on his face, "Sir, I don't understand. This is an all-inclusive ticket. It entitles you to three meals a day, anything from the menu, as much as you want for free."

There was so much available and yet in ignorance he had been content with so little.

At the Lord's Table there is so much available. His Table is plentiful. Grace is on the menu. Forgiveness is on the menu. Joy and peace are on the menu. Healing is on the menu. Blessing is on the menu. It is an all you can eat buffet, and the price has been paid, all you have to do is tuck in.

How can we be satisfied with so little of God, when there is so much available?

And yet even this is just a foretaste to the even greater Feast that we shall enjoy when we eat and drink with Him in His future Kingdom.

Do you long for that day? Can you join in with the Psalmist?

'How lovely is your dwelling-place, Lord Almighty! My soul yearns, even faints, for the courts of the Lord; my heart and my flesh cry out for the living God.'
(Psalm 84:1-2)

Or in the words of this modern day Psalm:

The more I seek You
The more I find You
The more I find You
The more I love You

I want to sit at Your feet
Drink from the cup in Your hand
Lay back against You and breathe
Feel your heart beat

This love is so deep
It's more than I can stand
I melt in Your peace
It's overwhelming

© 1999 Gateway Create Publishing, Integrity's Praise! Music

A Prayer of Response

"Jesus I am hungry and thirsty for You. I long for Your presence for it is only You that can satisfy. Let me receive afresh Your precious, life giving Holy Spirit. Oh, to drink of Your Spirit is truly wonderful. But even this is not enough. I long to see You face to face. I long for Your return. I long to dwell in Your house and sit at Your table forever. Oh, my heart and my flesh cry out for You God. My spirit and Your Spirit within me groan out this longing, "Come Lord Jesus, Come."

"This King, so full of mercy and goodness, very far from chastening me, embraces me with love, invites me to feast at His Table, serves me with His own hands, and gives me the key to His treasures. He converses with me, and takes great delight in me, and treats me as if I were His favourite."

- Brother Lawrence

CONCLUSION: THE MIRACLE TABLE

"You prepare a table before me in the presence of my enemies. You anoint my head with oil; my cup overflows. "

(Psalm 23:5)

Surely there are miracles available at the Lord's Table. As we approach the Lord's Table, we remind ourselves of the death of Christ on the Cross, on the blood that was shed, and in the words of Isaiah the prophet:

'Surely he took up our pain and bore our suffering, yet we considered him punished by God, stricken by him, and afflicted. But he was pierced for our transgressions, he was crushed for our iniquities; the punishment that brought us peace was on him, and by his wounds we are healed.' (Isaiah 53:4-5)

The word translated pain is the Hebrew word meaning illness, sickness, affliction, or wound. It is speaking of physical suffering in our bodies. This is what Jesus 'took up' - meaning to bear, or to carry away, and this is what we remind ourselves every time we take Communion.

A Roman flogging would have seen the victim lashed 39 times. Some medical experts have concluded there are 39 root causes to all the known diseases in the world. I can imagine the devil laughing and the demons rubbing their hands in glee at the suffering that the Son of God was going through. They should have read the Scriptures. Little did they know that as He was beaten and lashed, Jesus was fulfing the words of Isaiah that, 'By His wounds we are healed.'

At the Table I remind myself of the covenant that was made through the precious blood of Jesus. That covenant means that 'No matter how many promises God has made, they are "yes" in Christ.' (1 Corinthians 1:20)

Surely those promises include the declaration: 'I am the Lord who heals you.' (Exodus 15:26) And the wonderful truth that He is the God who 'Forgives all your sins and heals all your diseases.' (Psalm 103:3)

At the Table I eat and drink of His resurrection life, a life without weakness, sickness, disease, or decay. As I eat and drink of His life, I taste 'the powers of the coming age' in which death shall be no more, standing on the promise of Romans 8:11 that 'If the Spirit of Him that raised up Jesus from the dead dwell in you, He that raised up Christ from the dead shall also quicken your mortal bodies by His Spirit that dwelleth in you.'

If those that fail to discern the body of the Lord during Communion reap sickness, weakness, and death, (1 Corinthians 11) surely it stands to reason that those that take Communion and do discern the body of Christ shall receive healing, strength, and life.

In John 3, Jesus recalls the story in Numbers 21 of the Israelites being bitten by snakes - the venom entering their bodies and many of them dying. God said to Moses:

'"Make a snake and put it up on a pole; anyone who is bitten can look at it and live."

So Moses made a bronze snake and put it up on a pole. Then when anyone was bitten by a snake and looked at the bronze snake, they lived.' (Numbers 21:8)

Jesus compares the lifting of the snake to His own death on the cross. He says that just as the children of Israel gazed upon the snake on the pole and lived, now all who look to Him shall receive the life of God.

Surely as we come to the Table of the Lord, we gaze upon Jesus. We turn our focus and our attention upon Him. He becomes the source of our thanksgiving and worship. As we gaze upon Him, surely as it did to Israel, the healing power of God, and the very life of His Spirit will flow into our bodies.

There is an anointing at the Table. It is here that He anoints our head with oil. It is this anointing that breaks the yoke of sickness and disease. It is this anointing that enabled the Lord to heal all the sick that came to Him. (Matthew 8:16) This anointing has not changed, for He is the same yesterday, today, and forever. (Hebrews 13:8) And that anointing flows into our lives as we dine with Him at His Table.

In Matthew 15 there is a remarkable account of a Canaanite woman desperately needing a miracle from God. Her daughter is demon possessed and suffering terribly. As this woman is a Gentile, she is not at this moment a part of God's redemptive purposes, and the mission of Jesus. Because of this He seems to treat her harshly, initially saying nothing, and then seemingly calling her a dog.

Then she makes this incredible statement:

'Even the dogs eat the crumbs that fall from their master's table.' (v27)

Jesus response is immediate:

'"Woman, you have great faith! Your request is granted" And her daughter was healed at that moment.' (v28)

The woman is in effect saying, "I may be a dog in the eyes of the Jewish people, but dogs know what it is to come to the table, and eat the crumbs that fall. In the same way, I come to Your Table, and even if you give me just a crumb, that crumb is enough to heal, and deliver my daughter."

What a statement of faith! Surely we too can come to the Master's Table. As we eat of the bread that is on the Table, just one crumb is enough to heal, just one crumb is enough to deliver, just one crumb is enough the bring the miraculous power of God into every life, and every family.

Surly the crumbs that fall from the Master's Table are enough to heal cancer, to break depression, to deliver from addiction. Freedom, healing, deliverance, and the miraculous provision of God - it is all available at the Table.

The even greater news for us who are part of the New Covenant is that we do not approach the Table as dogs, but as dearly loved sons and daughters. According to Jesus, healing is the children's bread, (v26) and as His children we come to His Table and eat of the Bread that brings healing and life.

In Judges 6, Israel is being heavily oppressed by the Midianites. For seven years the Midianites steal, kill, and destroy from God's people. God raises up a deliverer named Gideon and one night he sneaks into the enemy's camp. There he hears one of the Midianites recounting a dream, 'A round loaf of barley bread came tumbling into the Midianite camp. It struck the tent with such force that the tent overturned and collapsed.' (Judges 7:13)

The interpretation of the dream is pretty clear: 'This can be nothing other than the sword of Gideon…God has given the Midianites and the whole camp into his hands.' (v14)

Like the Midianites, satan our adversary has oppressed many of us. He has attacked our health, our finances, our families. He has stolen our joy and peace.

And yet we have a Deliverer, and His Name is Jesus. As we come to the Communion table we remind our enemy of the Bread that destroyed the enemy's stronghold. That Bread that was broken, that Bread that was hung upon the tree, that Bread that was resurrected and lives forevermore. Surely that Bread has become for us a sword. Surely that Bread fights for us. Surely that Bread has broken the power of the enemy. There is victory in that Bread. There is life in that Bread.

The sign of the bread was a signal leading into one of the greatest miracles in the Bible, the defeat of the enemies of God, and the victory of Israel over their oppressor. Surely as we approach the Lord's Table we look to the greatest sign - the Bread of Life - Jesus. Through His death and resurrection, sickness and death have been defeated, and the miraculous power of God is freely available to all of God's children.

There is healing at the Table. There are miracles at the Table. Oh come, come and taste. Come taste and see that the Lord is good!

> 'I have no taste for the food that perishes nor for the pleasures of this life. I want the bread of God, which is the flesh of Christ; and for the drink I desire His blood, which is love that cannot be destroyed.'
> St. Ignatius of Antioch

"Recognise in this bread what hung on the cross, and in this chalice what flowed from His side"

- St Augustine

Afterword: Seeing Jesus

"Sir", they said, "we would like to see Jesus"

(John 12:21)

Surely as I approach the Table I see Jesus.

I see Him as:

God. The One who created me for a relationship

The Passover Lamb. The One who's blood was shed so that my sins could be forgiven

My Saviour. The One who delivers me from sin, death and hell

The Resurrection. The One who gives me life eternal

The Bread. The source of my life and strength. The One who satisfies my soul

The Wine. The One who has made a covenant with me to never leave me or forsake me. The One who gives me access to all of God's promises

The friend of sinners. The One who always welcomes me and accepts me no matter who I am or what I do

My High Priest. The One who is always there. The One who speaks His powerful blessing over my life

My Father. The One who adopts me and calls me His child

My King. The One who gives me victory over my enemies

The lover of my soul. The One who longs for a passionate, intimate relationship with me that is filled with joy and freedom

The Anointed One. The One who has power to heal sickness and disease and break the power of satan over my life

The builder of His Church. The One who invites me into family and community with all His people

My Lord and Master. The One I submit to and worship

The Bridegroom. The One who is coming again to take me to live in His presence forever

Oh, do you see Jesus? And not only do you see Him, but do you know Him? One of the disciples of Jesus, Peter had failed badly. He lied, cursed and denied knowing Jesus. We can only imagine the guilt and the shame that Peter felt.

But several days later on a beach, Jesus cooks Peter a meal (John 21). It is as they eat together that Peter realises that He has been forgiven and He is restored back into right relationship with his friend.

In John 11 another one of Jesus' friends, Lazarus gets sick and dies. Placed in a tomb for four days, His body has even begun to decay. But then appears Jesus. His mighty power raises Lazarus from the dead and in chapter 12 we see Lazarus dining with Jesus at His Table. From death, to decay to dining. This is the power of Jesus.

As Lazarus died so all of us are born dead in our sins. It is that sin that causes our lives to stink of guilt, shame and condemnation. It is that sin that separates us from God, places us in a tomb of darkness and leaves us lost and helpless. But we have a mighty Saviour! One who calls us out of darkness, out of death, out of sin and carries us to His Table where we can have relationship with Him.

Like Peter, no matter who we are or what we have done, Jesus wants to dine with us today. As we dine with Him we receive His forgiveness and He restores back to us our true identity as children of God.

The great evangelist Reinhard Bonnke says "At Holy Communion when the emblems of bread and wine are taken: what a prime opportunity to preach salvation. That cup of red wine is the greatest preacher in the world, to convict sinners of their sin. It is the gospel in a cup – an opportunity to invite lost sinners to accept the sacrifice of the Cross."

Will you respond to this invitation today? Pray with me.

'Lord Jesus, I know that I am a sinner and that I need a Saviour. I believe that you are that Saviour. I believe that you died and rose again. Today I receive Your free gift of Salvation. I repent of all my sin. Wash me and cleanse me with Your Precious blood. Adopt me into Your family. Make me Your child. I give my life to You. I receive Your gift of eternal life and I receive the life of Your Holy Spirit. Thank You for saving me. Amen'

"Here, O my Lord, I see thee face to face
Here would I touch and handle things unseen
Here grasp with firmer hand and eternal grace
And all my weariness upon Thee lean

Here would I feed upon the bread of God
Here drink with Thee the royal wine of Heaven
Here would I lay aside each earthly load
Here taste afresh the calm of sin forgiven

This is the hour of banquet and of song
This is the Heavenly table spread for me"

- Horatius Bonnet

About the Author

Andrew is the founder and director of Generation Builders and travels the world extensively as an evangelist, teacher and revivalist.

Born into a Christian family Andrew has been in full time Christian ministry since the age of eighteen. In September 2001 he began working full time at Royston Bethel Community Church in Barnsley, South Yorkshire. He remained on staff at the church for thirteen years serving initially as an intern and then later as a schools and youth worker.

During this time Andrew, achieved a certificate in Biblical studies from Mattersey Hall Bible College and later became a fully accredited minister with the Assemblies of God UK and Ireland.

In 2006, Andrew was appointed youth pastor and then later assistant pastor at Bethel Church, serving firstly under Pastor John Morgan and later Pastor Dave Jones.

In January 2007 Andrew had a powerful encounter with the Holy Spirit which led to a wonderful move of God in the youth group at the Church, with many young people coming and experiencing God's presence. This was the start of Andrew launching "Generation Builders" and beginning to travel to the nations.

In 2014 Andrew handed over his pastoral duties in the church and was released by the leadership to run Generation Builders full time. Since that time he has travelled the world seeing moves of God's Spirit marked by salvations, healings and thousands of people impacted by the preaching and teaching of God's Word.

Andrew is currently a member of and part of the ministry team at Revive Church, a multi-site church based in East Yorkshire led by Jarrod Cooper.

Andrew oversees Revive College, a training programme committed to raising up the next generation of revivalists by combining theological and leadership training with a missional experience in a Spirit filled community.

Andrew is married to Laura and they have two children Judah and Asher.

Contact Information

For more information about Generation Builders Ministries please visit our website www.generationbuilders.org

If you have been blessed by this book or are interested in having Andrew Murray speak at your church or event then please email admin@generationbuilders.org

For more information about Revive College please visit our website or email college@revivechurch.co.uk

For more information about Peanut Designs please visit www.pnutd.co.uk

SEEING THE CHURCH

WHEN YOUR PURPOSE COLLIDES WITH GOD'S PASSION

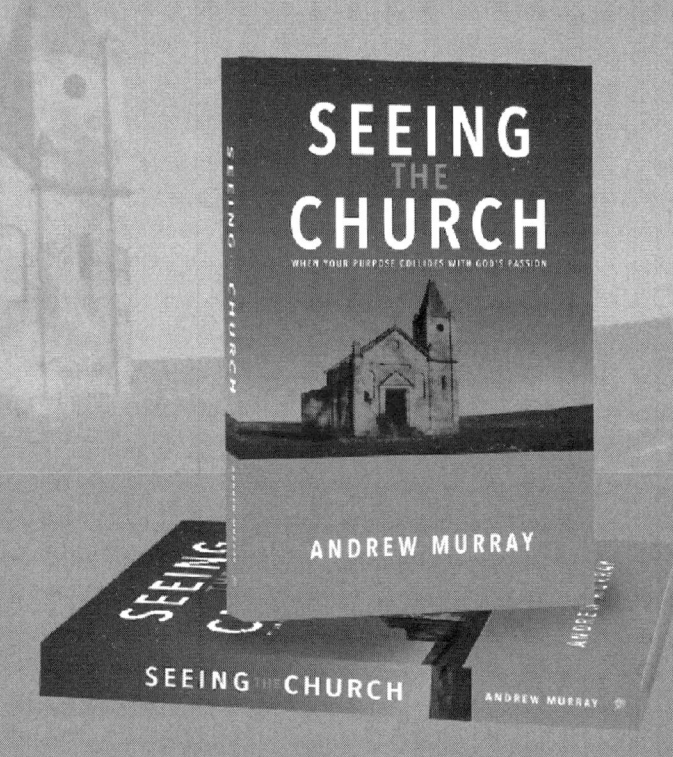

ANDREW MURRAY

Available on
amazon & kindle

Printed in Great Britain
by Amazon